# BASIC TEXTS IN COUNSELLING AND PSYCHOTHERAPY

Series editor: Stephen Frosh

This series introduces readers to the theory and practice of counselling and psychotherapy across a wide range of topic areas. The books will appeal to anyone wishing to use counselling and psychotherapeutic skills and are particularly relevant to workers in health, education, social work and related settings. The books are unusual in being rooted in psychodynamic and systemic ideas, yet being written at an accessible, readable and introductory level. Each text offers theoretical background and guidance for practice, with creative use of clinical examples.

*Published*

Jenny Altschuler
WORKING WITH CHRONIC ILLNESS

Bill Barnes, Sheila Ernst and Keith Hyde
AN INTRODUCTION TO GROUPWORK

Stephen Briggs
WORKING WITH ADOLESCENTS

Alex Coren
SHORT-TERM PSYCHOTHERAPY

Emilia Dowling and Gill Gorell Barnes
WORKING WITH CHILDREN AND PARENTS THROUGH SEPARATION AND DIVORCE

Loretta Franklin
AN INTRODUCTION TO WORKPLACE COUNSELLING

Gill Gorell Barnes
FAMILY THERAPY IN CHANGING TIMES – 2e

Sally Hodges
COUNSELLING ADULTS WITH LEARNING DISABILITIES

Ravi Rana
COUNSELLING STUDENTS

Geraldine Shipton
WORKING WITH EATING DISORDERS

Tricia Scott
INTEGRATIVE PSYCHOTHERAPY IN HEALTH CARE

Paul Terry
COUNSELLING THE ELDERLY AND THEIR CARERS

Jan Wiener and Mannie Sher
COUNSELLING AND PSYCHOTHERAPY IN PRIMARY HEALTH CARE

Shula Wilson
DISABILITY, COUNSELLING AND PSYCHOTHERAPY

Laurence Spurling
AN INTRODUCTION TO PSYCHODYNAMIC COUNSELLING

Invitation to authors

The Series Editor welcomes proposals for new books within the Basic Texts in Counselling and Psychotherapy series. These should be sent to Stephen Frosh at the School of Psychology, Birkbeck College, Malet Street, London, WCIE 7HX (email s.frosh@bbk.ac.uk).

**Basic Texts in Counselling and Psychotherapy**
**Series Standing Order ISBN 0–333–69330–2**
*(outside North America only)*

You can receive future titles in this series as they are published by placing a standing order. Please contact your bookseller or, in the case of difficulty, write to us at the address below with your name and address, the title of the series and the
ISBN quoted above.

Customer Services Department, Macmillan Distribution Ltd.
Houndmills, Basingstoke, Hampshire RG21 6XS, England

# WORKING WITH EATING DISORDERS

## A Psychoanalytic Approach

GERALDINE SHIPTON

First published 2004 by
PALGRAVE MACMILLAN
Houndmills, Basingstoke, Hampshire RG21 6XS and
175 Fifth Avenue, New York, N.Y. 10010
Companies and representatives throughout the world

PALGRAVE MACMILLAN is the global academic imprint of the Palgrave Macmillan division of St. Martin's Press, LLC and of Palgrave Macmillan Ltd. Macmillan® is a registered trademark in the United States, United Kingdom and other countries. Palgrave is a registered trademark in the European Union and other countries.

ISBN 0–333–99938–X paperback

This book is printed on paper suitable for recycling and made from fully managed and sustained forest sources.

A catalogue record for this book is available from the British Library.

A catalog record for this book is available from the Library of Congress.

10  9  8  7  6  5  4  3  2  1
13 12 11 10 09 08 07 06 05 04

Printed in China

# CONTENTS

CONTENTS

# ACKNOWLEDGEMENTS

I would like to thank all those people who have trusted me with accounts of their own eating difficulties and struggles with self-esteem and self-image. I hope I have used the privilege with due care and respect. I am especially grateful to Gianna Williams and members of the eating disorders workshop at the Adolescent Unit of the Tavistock Clinic. I have also learned a lot from all those participants who came on short courses in Sheffield or those who have spared time to talk to me since, such as Sandra Thomas. Em Farrell's contributions to the course as a seminar leader greatly aided my understanding of bulimia, in particular and made working together fun. Many others have contributed to the development of my understanding in different ways at different times. I thank Dr Anderson, Dr Birksted-Breen and Dr Sedlak for what they have taught me about psychoanalysis. I am grateful to Professor Ron Akehurst for study leave from the University of Sheffield and to Trudy Coldwell for her secretarial assistance. Finally, I thank AKB for his unstinting and essential support!

# 1

# INTRODUCTION

Eating disorders are one of the most common forms of mental health problem and are associated with increased risk to life. Over the last 30 years they have become more finely differentiated so that nowadays we talk of anorexia nervosa, bulimia nervosa, binge-eating, sub-acute eating disorders, eating disorders not otherwise specified (EDNOS) or may refer to obesity and self-starvation. We no longer believe anorexics are not hungry or that they are only ever young, white, middle-class females. Indeed, we are very well informed about eating disorders: our magazines and newspapers are full of information about the dangers of eating disorders and fascinated by the body-size of celebrities and the diets to which they subscribe. Obesity has become a major priority for governments across the world and according to the World Health Organisation is 'the single biggest European public health challenge of the 21st century' (Wallop, 2003) and may necessitate taxing fatty and sugary foods. Diets are big business, the fast food industry even bigger, and increasingly, so is litigation. Obese people have begun to sue food companies and retailers such as McDonalds for apparently making them obese. Eating disorders bring together the private and the public in a very profitable way. And furthermore, we all know what it feels like to question whether or not we are eating 'properly' or look 'right'.

Eating is an activity that involves the external and the internal world. Menzies summed this up as: 'One may truly say people never eat alone or uninfluenced by others, since they always eat in the context of the "internal society"' (Menzies, 1970: 223). This internal society is made up of the relationships we experienced when young but further external influences cannot be avoided whether we wish them to be or not and we are all subject to external judgement about what are acceptable or unacceptable ways of dealing with our earlier feeding experiences. Menzies reminds us of a scene from one of the films, 'John', made by the Robertsons (1969), in a residential nursery. In it we see children stealing food from each other even though food is plentiful. What is scarce is a stable relationship to a good, loving adult: a mother substitute which is lost to them, so they fight for the food that represents her instead. Menzies tells us that mothers also use food, for example, to deal with separation by giving their children food to take to school with them while they themselves may deal with loneliness and boredom at home by feeding themselves. She links rituals around food and drink with reconciliation – the repair of a good society, sitting down and eating together. Some readers may remember the advertising campaign for 'Cadbury's Snack' which had a jingle 'Bridge that gap with Cadbury's snack!' The gap, Menzies pointed out, was a relationship gap not a food gap (Menzies, 1970: 225). This idea sums up the basis of the book: it aims to consider the different ways in which eating and not eating compensate for an absence of an emotional and relational kind, and the conflicts which might ensue.

## The incidence of eating disorders

According to the National Service Framework for the National Health Service (NHS), the most common mental health problems are depression, eating disorders and anxiety disorders (DOH, 1999: 32) yet only 48 per cent of health authorities have local specialist services and access to services is unevenly spread across the country. The mortality rate is very high for eating disorders (see Royal College of Psychiatrists, 2000: 68), falling behind only the rates for prescription drugs and illegal drug abuse, opioid abuse, mental retardation (sic) and suicide attempt by self-poisoning. The south east of England has 60 per cent of consultant psychiatry sessions dedicated to eating disorders, yet it only has 33 per cent of the population (see Royal College of Psychiatrists, 2000). The lack of provision and seriousness of the nature of the problems has led the Royal College to call for more provision and more specialist training. Although the emphasis is, appropriately, on their own profession, there are many other practitioners in the NHS, in student counselling, and in the private sector, who are challenged by the nature of the difficulties such patients present. Student counselling services in particular are likely to see a wide range and very large numbers of people who want help with an eating disorder.

# Eating disorders as an end-point for different pathological processes

Stephen L. Post, in a panel discussion of a meeting of the American Psychoanalytic Association (discussed in Castelnuovo-Tedesco and Whisnant Reiser, 1988: 167) noted that all the papers that were presented there on eating disorders showed a fundamental interrelatedness between anorexia, bulimia and obesity. However, he did not consider them to have enough in common to be viewed as on a continuum, despite additional shared body-image preoccupations. He drew attention to the local, historical and economic influences on obesity. One linking theme was impulsivity. However, others have commented on how an eating disorder may be an expression of varying degrees and levels of pathology from an underlying potential psychosis, through to a borderline personality disorder, a neurotic disposition or a fleeting transitional problem in adolescence. It is also the case that as eating is a basic human function it is also affected by most major changes as it is in depression, for example, or hypomania. Anorexia, when it is simply a physical symptom, can be caused by a range of problems, not necessarily psychological, which is why when it is part of an eating disorder it is often called anorexia nervosa, in order to distinguish it. I have sometimes used anorexia as a term on its own because within the context of this book it is clearly the eating disorder which is indicated, but at other times I have employed the full term. Similarly, I have used the term bulimia or bulimia nervosa interchangeably. Seeing patients for psychotherapy over fairly substantial periods of time has also alerted me to the fact that many people who suffer from a difficulty in later years have had an eating disorder which has gone unnoticed when they were young, especially at adolescence or early adulthood.

As more has been written about working successfully with people with an eating disorder and as the influence of self-help groups and the women's health movement has diminished, there has been a professionalisation of help offered. Although enormously important organisations such as the Eating Disorders Association (EDA) have helped people with a problem and their close associates, there has been an increase in specialised eating disorder units and services. There are now specialist training courses on eating disorders including a Masters Degree at the Tavistock Clinic.

## Children with eating disorders

The book does not go into the eating disorders as they are found in childhood: this would be a whole book in itself. In some quarters in the USA, childhood eating disorders like anorexia are thought of as 'a developmental disorder of separation and individuation' (Chatoor and Egon, 1983; Chatoor, 1991). By contrast, in Britain there is also a tradition which emphasises the role of unconscious phantasy. The work carried out at the Tavistock Clinic with adolescents and children is mentioned later in the book and for further insights into their approach, in which the work of Bion is especially pertinent, readers might want to refer to Anderson and Dartington (1998) and Williams (1997).

## Men with eating disorders

The overwhelming majority of people with eating disorders are heterosexual women. It is not clear how many men have eating disorders, but a figure commonly quoted is that an estimated 10 per cent of all cases of eating disorders are male. As 60 000–90 000 people with eating disorders are referred to clinics at any one time in the UK, this suggests that between 6000 and 9000 men should be considering or receiving treatment. However, for a variety of reasons this seems not to be the case. Gender and sexuality appear to be significant factors, with approximately 20 per cent of men with eating disorders identifying themselves as gay, double the estimated proportion of gay men in the population. The reasons for these divergences in gender and sexuality are debatable and will be considered in later chapters. All these statistics come from a report written for the Eating Disorders Association by Jeanette Copperman (2000) which found that not enough was being done to explore and address the specific treatment needs of men with eating disorders. One clear problem was access to services and a tendency of some clinicians to view anorexia and bulimia, in particular, as 'women's problems' therefore they did not diagnose them accurately when they were present in male patients. The criteria for recognising anorexia, for example, include consideration of whether menstruation has ceased. There is no equivalent for men. I have concentrated mainly on women with eating disorders in this book because my experience is overwhelmingly with women patients but I hope some of its contents will be helpful in working with men, since in the report mentioned, patients and professionals alike found that there was an 'overlap' of issues. There is, however, a short section on men with eating disorders and their particular problems with gender identity and body image in Chapter 6.

## Moving in a psychoanalytic direction

The orientation developed in this book is object relations. When I began working with eating disordered patients I was not qualified as a psychotherapist but had some counselling, group, and creative therapy training from my occupational therapy background. I was also undertaking family therapy training, and was inspired by Minuchin's book *'Psychosomatic Families: Anorexia Nervosa in Context'*. My interest shifted to the work of the Women's Therapy Centre (WTC) in London because of the way they were able to combine therapeutic insights and an analysis of how society impacted on the individual psyche and the family system. The slogan 'the personal is political' expressed the zeitgeist and the feelings of a generation of men and women who wanted to bring about radical change in many different areas of life. I went to events at WTC and helped to organise workshops locally, and therapists from WTC came north to demonstrate the way they worked. Workshop leaders like Mira Dana, Marilyn Lawrence and others utilised a psychoanalytic as well as a feminist approach. I was inspired and decided to train formally as a psychotherapist. I have thus evolved as a therapist in a culture influenced by radicalism as well as psychoanalysis, and by systemic as well as individual approaches to change. There is a considerable role for family therapy and group therapy in the treatment of people with eating disorders and their families but the focus here is on an individual approach, although group therapy is mentioned briefly in Chapter 4.

Much of the American literature on Eating Disorders proceeded from a reaction to a classical kind of psychoanalysis which favoured an emphasis on interpreting drives in a fairly implacable way (though this may be more a stereotype of bad, rather than classical psychoanalysis). Hilda Bruch advanced an alternative way of responding to anorexics in particular, which challenged the classical approach. The American self-psychologists advanced yet another framework in reaction to some of the limitations of her work. It is a research and clinical field which has been extensively investigated and theorised.

As I have developed, moving from the NHS to working in a student counselling setting, then becoming a psychotherapist in private practice and an academic, I have found the ideas in object relations theory to be very helpful in making sense of working with eating disorders in various settings. I hope this book will help others who share my interests, and that the limited range of theory offered will not duplicate too much of what is already familiar to them. What I trust is that the concepts and technique I have found useful and the clinical experiences that have shaped my views may be of benefit to others. The aim is not to try to map out the whole gamut of eating disorders, theory, technique, aetiology and cultural dimensions. Instead, I propose to focus on a psychoanalytic perspective which opens up several possibilities for understanding and treating eating disorders, agreeing with Hamburg that: 'The "deconstruction" of a symptom seeks to restore the complexity concealed in its construction' (Hamburg, 1989: 137).

## Who is this book for?

This book is intended for anyone who works psychotherapeutically with people with eating disorders. Not everyone who does this work has undertaken a coherent psychoanalytic or psychodynamic training. For example, many clinical psychologists work with people with eating disorders, and they may have been trained in a broad and eclectic way. However, the insights from psychoanalytic theory are so rich it seems to me that they can be used to illuminate a range of clinical material, dealing as they do with unconscious processes that affect both practitioner and patient or client. In a book such as this one, there is not the space for a thorough discussion of the different definitions that have been employed to distinguish psychoanalysis from psychotherapy or psychotherapy from counselling. However, it is helpful to draw out one or two implications for readers. In this book, whoever is doing the clinical work and with whatever training, it is taken for granted that they are not seeing patients or clients for more than once- or twice-a-week therapy. While frequency of sessions alone is not an indicator of the kind of work going on in them, it is nonetheless true, that the possibility of exploring and working through conflicts is hampered if time has not been put aside for the therapeutic couple to give themselves over to a free associative process. In the full analytic process, the priority is for the patient to understand him or herself. The analyst does not know or yet fully understand, and is a partner in the journey of exploration with the patient. In psychotherapy, it might be more the job of the therapist to offer ways of understanding to the patient (see Spillius, 2002: 5). This puts greater pressure on the therapist to be able to hold the patient from one session to the next. In counselling, I am assuming a general tendency to follow the external realities of which the client speaks more closely than in psychotherapy, and where the client is less likely to be able to regress (see Shipton and Smith, 1998: 9–26 for a fuller attempt at distinguishing counselling from psychotherapy). For the purposes of this book, it seems rather unhelpful to get too closely involved in the intricacies of differentiating one practice from another, and almost certainly will end up alienating someone who feels misrepresented by my inadequate efforts.

The main point is that this book is not a guide to working as a psychoanalyst but is informed and inspired by both psychoanalytic theory and practice. Readers are invited to take what they can from it but in the sure knowledge that it can only be useful if insights can be integrated successfully with their own way of practising.

## The structure of the book

This introduction is followed by Chapter 2 which situates the nosological category of eating disorder in a much wider cultural context. The chapter starts with a brief history of eating itself so as to prepare the ground for the premise that there is no 'normal' eating pattern which is universal and consistent over time, and especially to avoid the mistaken belief that eating has traditionally been a private matter. The way in which the female body in particular has been affected is mentioned. Feminists have criticised patriarchal culture in relation to oppressive practices towards the body and the mind. The pioneering work of several feminists is referred to, some are clinicians and psychoanalytic, others more interested in developing a critique of contemporary cultural representations of the female body and eating. Anorexia in particular has been viewed almost as a 'star' pathology with some commentators seeing a lineage going right back to antiquity. Some of the difficulties in this backwards reading into history are contemplated. The role of dieting, self-management and embodiment in general is discussed from a more sociological slant. Finally, the vexed question of the role of culture in the creation of pathological eating disorders and in less acute problems with eating and body image is considered. The belief that an 'epidemic' of eating disorders is spreading across the globe to less affluent parts of the world is assessed. The issue of globalisation and the cultural context is also returned to briefly in Chapter 7.

Having outlined a historical and ideological background, there are then three chapters which are more clinically orientated. Chapter 3 is concerned with anorexia and describes several criteria which are used for diagnostic purposes and presents a range of theories about its aetiology. There are several clinical vignettes and one major case-study. The notion that anorexia may be linked to bulimia is central to the argument outlined. The clinical work, which is portrayed in some detail, is mainly related to starting psychotherapy with an anorexic patient. It draws on the extensive literature which suggests that creating a safe holding environment and an internal space for potential emotional digestion are absolute necessities for engaging anorexic people in the psychotherapeutic process. The issue of fear of intrusion is highlighted and set against the essential loneliness of many anorexics who may also wish not to feel isolated. There is also a brief description of a therapy which broke down, and a more successful but short-term therapeutic encounter with an anorexic student.

A similar pattern is followed in Chapter 4, starting with the problem of what to include under the heading bulimia and whether or not to incorporate aspects of the literature on anorexia. Some of the various ways in which bulimia has been understood in the past (that is since 1979, when it became clinically distinguished from some kinds of anorexia by psychiatrists) are mentioned, as well as more contemporary views. The propensity for some bulimics to be conceived of as having borderline personality disorder features of pathology is considered. There then follows a brief vignette about a young bulimic man who could not be satisfactorily contained in a group. Finally, there is a description of the most salient features of a once-a-week psychotherapy of a woman over five years.

Chapter 5 takes up the subject of obesity and compulsive eating. This category of eating disorder has been linked with non-psychological/psychiatric medicine historically, and the reasons for this are discussed. The story is told of a brief encounter with an extremely obese woman, and it is argued that listening and counselling skills, though not sufficient to bring about any change in such a patient, may help the patient sustain a belief in a therapeutic alliance which could be entered into at a deeper level in the future. The limited psychoanalytic literature about obesity is then reiterated. A long, twice-a-week therapy with a person who was overweight and who continued to increase her weight for part of her therapy is reflected upon, in the light of the theory.

The clinical examples given throughout the book are heavily disguised to protect the identity of the individuals concerned. Where it has been possible to get permission from patients to write about them I have done so and where not, for reasons such as change of address or no address, I have composited various characters as well as disguising some features which could identify people. Experience has taught me that people will identify with material that does not come from a real patient, and are sometimes shocked by the extent to which it feels familiar to them. I once invented a clinical scenario when running a large workshop in order to demonstrate a particular point. One participant spoke movingly about how I had just described how he felt at one point in his life but he did not think to tell the rest of the group that I had never met him before.

Chapter 6 picks up on some of the important issues that clinicians need to think about in relation to eating disorders and begins with the problems in starting therapy with someone. When assessing patients there is a need to be sensitive to both the problem in helping them give up what might feel like a solution to their problems and their terror of feeling more out of control or exposed as fundamentally unacceptable. The debate about whether or not psychoanalytic approaches to working with eating disorders are appropriate or should be modified, or indeed, are counter-indicated is explored briefly and some thought given to the challenge an eating disordered person makes to the analytic stance of neutrality. Body image is then discussed and what it might represent in men, in particular, is considered. The chapter ends with a reiteration of the value of good supervision, not just for formal psychotherapy and therapeutic counselling, but for professionals whose role may be auxiliary to therapy but who can become very stirred up by projections from patients.

Chapter 7 gathers together some of the psychoanalytic concepts that readers may find valuable in thinking about their work. These include psychic retreats, psychotic parts of the mind, symbolic equation, negation and mental space. There is then a brief consideration of other factors that may be important for some patients with eating disorders. These are: psychosomatic disorders, in particular Irritable Bowel Syndrome, self-harm and sexual abuse. The role of self-help is mentioned and the delicate nature of helping families and friends of people with eating disorders where the patient is reluctant to seek professional help is discussed. Some thoughts about research are given and the issue of the cultural context of eating disorders is revisited.

Each of the chapters is rounded off with a list of key points for consideration and discussion where appropriate. At the end of the book are notes referred to in the text and addresses or websites which readers may find useful and a full list of references.

# 2

# THE CULTURAL CONTEXT OF EATING DISORDERS

The connections between the society we live in and the roles we are expected to play in it clearly affect how we think about ourselves and how we behave. However, the specific ways in which culture, in its most general meaning, affects the individual's unconscious is impossible to predict with certainty. Yet advertising makes an assumption that it can influence us with some degree of accuracy: who amongst us has not looked at the billboards which advertise products adorned by a very slender, scantily clad woman and not thought 'what is that telling us about how women should look and about what we should want?'. We can analyse the messages and the images but we cannot be sure how they are read or received. Some of us will buy the products advertised, some of us will diet to look like the model and others amongst us might resolve not to buy *that* brand of vodka or jeans. It quite simply varies! We have a choice about how we react. Nonetheless, eating disorders are believed to be on the increase and many commentators have puzzled about why that should be so. Fonagy cautioned: '... we are rarely able to comment meaningfully on demographic trends such as recent increases in the prevalence of eating disorders or the varying prevalence of disorders across the life-span ...' (Fonagy, 1999).

Many previous writers have tried to make some links with social processes in understanding eating disorders. In particular, there is a history of a feminist perspective, which has aimed not to split women who seek help from the rest of the female population for whom the body and food are an everyday preoccupation. Pioneering American feminists of the late twentieth century, like Chernin, and Bordo, and feminists based in Britain, like Orbach, Eichenbaum, Lawrence and others, have highlighted some common themes about how society relates to the female body. I will briefly consider these and more contemporary perspectives before mentioning the sociology of embodiment. I will then return to the belief that eating disorders are on the increase and that they have special significance for women. Any approach to thinking about cultural dimensions of clinical problems must take into account the small number of men (an estimated 10 per cent of sufferers) who develop eating disorders. But first of all I want to sketch out a brief history of eating.

## A short history of eating

Eating has become an area of private, individual choice and public debate. There is a history to this now privatised activity and to its investment with individual meanings in relation to the self. Falk (1994) linked the body, the self and culture through a study of consumption. Falk outlined what has been considered edible or inedible in the past, and demonstrated how this has given way to the modern capitalist notion of 'goods' which we are encouraged to consume for a self-relating experience. Our modern self is understood as an individual entity possessing an inside and an outside, constituted by the body. In primitive society the environment of the body is only one kind of 'inside'. The other surface is turned towards nature or others who are not like 'us'. In primitive society eating is a community activity – the body is open to the community – the group has a say in it. The body could be said to be constituted by sharing. The original primitive symbiosis of the mother–baby dyad develops into a community-bond, which is renewed by sharing the same food with companions (this last word is derived from the Latin for 'with bread': com + panis). When the eating-community collapses, eating is affected: the 'open' body, which is affiliated to the group, becomes a 'closed' body, over which only the individual then exercises control. Heightened self-control over the body space creates an imaginary inwardness for emotional experience. Wouters (1977) says that the eating-community became replaced by a talking-socialising community and thus eating became one-sided: about taking in food, not about the group taking in the eating individual. Eating itself became problematised in a personal way with consequences such as the development of pathological constructs like overeating or gluttony and 'unhealthy' practices of body or mind. Such problems then required a disciplining of appetite (Mennell, 1985).

Falk tells us: 'The closing of the body creates an empty inside – both in physical and mental terms – to be filled up with all the good things it lacks' (1994: 28). Thus we see the beginnings of the modern individual self: a separate being with an inside to be filled up and waiting to be completed. The upshot of the argument is that communion gave way to communication and the ethos of modern culture in which people relate to themselves and to separate others and to objects of consumption.

A general concept of the body has only emerged in the last few centuries. Relationship between the animate and non-animate body was once key. The soul was the subtraction, which came out of the two: the basis of the sacred–profane dichotomy. Yet at the outset body and soul were not two parallel entities. Early on, the soul was thought to be in the blood. Under Christianity, the body was seen negatively. From Augustine onwards sins became important. These were linked in a causal chain: gluttony encouraged lust and fornication, which generated greed and anger, leading to sadness and sloth. Vainglory and pride were also considered sins but these were not body based.

The body became construed as the prisoner of the soul (Foucault, 1979: 30). Soul now transformed the body into a medium for action based on rational will and concerned with furthering personal interests. Passions and vices became more firmly connected with natural tendencies to be struggled with in the body. By way of contrast, in the Middle Ages the three main sins were lust for money and ownership, lust for power and lust for sexual flesh. Eventually the body became synonymous with the self. In eating disorders, some of which have been construed as 'Disorders of the Self' (see Strober, 1991), it has been mainly the female body which has been the focus of attention. It is to the female body that I now wish to turn.

## Some feminist perspectives on eating disorders

It is not surprising that eating disorders have been taken up as a feminist issue since exposing the relationship of oppression, in various forms, to the vicissitudes of the female body has been one of the hallmarks of feminist activism. As long ago as 1792, Mary Wollstonecroft wrote 'Women are everywhere in this deplorable state … Taught from their infance that beauty is woman's sceptre, the mind shapes itself to the body, and, roaming around its gilt cage, only seeks to adorn its prison' (in Bordo, 1993a: 186). Bordo tells us how Hilde Bruch's landmark work *Eating Disorders*, published in 1973, made little use of the concept of gender. Kim Chernin (1985) was one of the first to point out that the anorexic's body was almost always a female body, and what the anorexic seemed to be resisting was developing into a woman. Since then there has been a veritable tide of writing about eating disorders from a feminist angle. Gender had been either absent or theorised in essentialist terms according to Bordo until a conference called in 1983 on 'Eating Disorders and the Psychology of Women' in New York set out to rectify this situation. Feminists, who had been active outside the traditional medical frameworks, often working in the women's self-help movement and consciousness raising groups, challenged the pathologisation of women with eating disorders and linked their problems to the dominant patriarchal culture. Susie Orbach argued at this conference that eating disorders reflected the cultural construction of femininity. She thought that all women were subject to psychological, social and economic pressures which compounded each other and made many women feel both miserable about their bodies and undermined in terms of power. This applied to therapists as well as patients. Orbach's stand was revolutionary. She linked anorexia, in particular, with a protest against woman's condition in the world, she questioned the validity of pathologisation of eating disorders, and she painted the clinician's self into the picture.

Since that time there has been a powerful movement of women, and some men, seeking to understand the phenomenon of eating disorders from a non-medical, critical perspective. Some were also clinicians like Orbach, who, like her, helped set up Women's Therapy Centres and Health Groups across Britain and the USA. Politicised books about health became best sellers: Orbach's *'Fat is a Feminist Issue'* (1978), *'Hunger Strike: The Anorectic's Struggle as a Metaphor for Our Age'* (1986); Ernst and Goodison's *'In Our Own Hands'* (1981); Lawrence's *'The Anorexic Experience'* (1984), *'Fed Up and Hungry: Women, Oppression and Food'* (1987). Similarly, in the USA, a plethora of books came out that inspired readers, especially Chernin's *'Womansize: Reflections on the Tyranny of Slenderness'* (1983) and *'The Hungry Self: Women, Eating and Identity'* (1985). The 1960s, 1970s and early 1980s were stirring times: the women's movement not only analysed the cultural dimensions of eating disorders but it radicalised people who suffered from them and got them involved in finding solutions to them. This cultural situating of eating disorders has gradually become absorbed into mainstream health care and the British-based women therapists just mentioned have become highly respected world-class experts on eating disorders with a psychodynamic as well as a feminist perspective. But the radical edge, the political dynamism and organisation have almost collapsed. Self-help groups are, perhaps still important, but they rattle no cages.

Political correctness and individualism have filled the gap where collective action used to predominate. It could be said that the professional 'talking cure' has also filled some of that space.

## Anorexia's special attraction

One eating disorder in particular has been taken up by contemporary cultural commentators, and that is anorexia nervosa. Malson (1998) has plotted out a genealogy of anorexia nervosa, following the method of Foucault, the French philosopher whose work has been extremely influential in social and feminist theory. She has examined the linking function that she perceives anorexia to play between the categories 'pathology' and 'women'. While some writers have claimed a continuous though long-forgotten history of anorexia dating back to the third century (Sours, 1980), many have cautioned against reading twenty-first century meanings into diversely motivated phenomena. Such a range of so-called predecessors to anorexics include St Wilgerfortis, who starved herself in the tenth century as a protest against being married off to a brutal Sicilian King (she succeeded, though her father had her crucified instead); a young depressed prince treated by the Persian physician, Avicenna in the eleventh century; and the so-called 'holy anorexics', described by Bell (1985), who fasted their way to sainthood in the Middle Ages. One famous example of these was Catherine of Sienna whose self-starvation and self-castigation seem to have been sought in a state of ecstatic devotion. 'Hunger artists' in late nineteenth-century Europe displayed themselves as part of their starvation performance art. Hunger strikers like the suffragettes at the turn of the last century, Gandhi, and the Irish Republican hunger strikers are more recent examples of an apparently related phenomenon, though their struggles were overtly political. These acts of starvation meant something different to the societies in which they were produced than eating disorders do to us today. However, themes of self-assertion, protest, defiance, spiritual superiority and self-realisation all crop up in explanations about anorexia in contemporary approaches.

However, Malson argued that anorexia nervosa did not exist already 'out there' waiting for doctors to diagnose it, before Gull or Lasegue claimed it in 1873 and planted the flag of hysteria upon it. Anorexia is a product, an outcome of the medical discourse of the nineteenth century onwards, she suggested. In her Foucauldian approach it is to the discourse and discursive practices which constitute anorexia that she turned to for greater understanding of its aetiology. She wrote

> … anorexia emerged at the interface of medical and cultural discourses on hypochondria, hysteria and femininity. It was constituted as a feminine nervous disorder at a time when the 'nervous woman' was a significant cultural figure … Anorexia thus figured as a political forum, as much as a medical one, in which to debate and therefore constitute and reconstitute feminine nervousness. (Malson, 1998: 49)

Although Malson saw no continuity of personal experience or social meaning reaching from 'fasting girls' like Catherine of Sienna to the present day, she notes the way that transition from a religious discourse to a medical one involved a shift from a theological interpretation of self-starvation to a 'scientific' medical theory about it. What she found in analysing discourses about anorexia was that the thin/anorexic body signified 'a multiplicity of subjectivities' and in trying to understand the discourse and practices which regulate feminine experience she discovered that 'Western culture was … deeply and complexly imbricated' in anorexic practices (Malson, 1998: 193).

## Eating disorders and self-management

Other feminists have employed alternative concepts derived from Foucault to elucidate the construction of femininity. Bordo mentions Foucault's notion of 'an agonistic relation with the self' aimed at combating weakness and mastering desire, a remnant of Ancient Greek thinking, but unbuckled from a context in which moderation was also valued highly. As Bordo says in today's world: '… as consumers we must display a boundless capacity to capitulate to desire and indulge in impulse; we must hunger for constant and immediate satisfaction' (1993b: 199). Bordo has analysed the multifarious signs and messages communicated to women in advertising. She concludes that the slender body represents the ideal of a well-managed self in which everything is under control despite the contradictions of our consumer culture exhorting us to be disciplined, hard-working, and to restrict food intake by day while we dedicate our nights and weekends to 'letting go': eating, drinking, shopping, drug-taking, TV goggling. Bordo sees bulimia as representing the characteristic personality type of our day who fulfils the requirements of consumer capitalism but it is a sort of double-bind that guarantees dissatisfaction. She sees the co-existence of anorexia and obesity as indicating how unstable the personality produced is: there is no permanent balance between the producer and the consumer sides of the self. Anorexia can then be seen as an extreme type of self-denial and management of desire, or 'the work ethic in absolute control'. Obesity can be seen as an extreme type of letting go or 'consumerism in control' (ibid.). No strategy for managing the self really works in our consumer society and we get into the habit of constant self-monitoring and adjusting to the shifting prevailing norms.

## Body practices and embodiment

Foucault's analysis of power relations takes us away from visualising power as held by people or groups, like a possession, towards the idea that power operates by a network of non-centralised forces which are constituted by the economic and ideological forms of a historical period. We can imagine, for example, the rise of the factory-age and the need to produce a workforce which is adapted to the machine. Such networks are not designed from above but are ushered in by a dynamic process which has different origins and sources, and which operates by elements of the construction of time, space, desire and embodiment. One mechanism which orchestrates this impersonal process is self-surveillance and self-correction to fit the individual to prevailing norms through a discipline of the self and the body. There is thus no pre-cultural or trans-historical feminine body, but discourses and practices which produce the body as a site and expression of power-relations, which correspond to the particular time and place.

Brian Turner developed a sociology of embodiment, rather than of the body, based to some extent on a critique of Foucault's work and its emphasis on the discourses which structure thinking about the body, but taking special note of the historical relationship between religion and the body (Turner, [1984] 1996). He stressed the lived experience of bodily practices, performed in social space as opposed to a reification of the body as a thing-in-itself, and formulated the notion of a 'somatic society' in which 'major political and personal problems are both problematised in the body and expressed through it' (Turner, 1996: 1). The body, in our current epoch of late capitalism and its promises of pleasure through consumption 'emerges as a field of hedonistic practices and desire in a culture which recognises that the body is a project' (Turner, 1996: 4). The post-modern self is closely linked with the development of consumerism and to desire, saturated with fantasies of unlimited consumption of material goods, food and signs. The self as a major project (and the talking cure is very much a part of the project along with other confessional schemes) has given way to the pre-eminence of the desiring body. Technology has contributed a promise of eternal plasticity and therefore endless possibility. However, Turner holds on to a view of the body which maintains that, although it is a socially constructed metaphor – the 'natural body' is always already a cultural and historical phenomenon – there are also ontologically given aspects to bodies (he gives left/right-handedness as an example). In other words, the body is both natural and cultural. Using the concept of bodily practices enables us to approach embodiment phenomenologically and yet take account of how it is socially and historically constructed. Turner set the stage for an exploration of the communal and collective nature of embodiment, while clinicians have tended to find particular and special instances of individual trajectories of personalisation and embodiment in work with patients.

> ... bodies are objects over which we labour – eating, sleeping, cleaning, dieting exercising. These labours can be called body practices and they are both individual and collective. These practices tie us into the natural world, since our bodies are environments, while also locating us into a dense system of social norms and regulations. ... the body is both an environment we practise and also practise with. ... (1996: 185)

The production of an anorexic body with its own special relation to space is the product of much labour in terms of dieting, exercise and self-surveillance. There is nothing abstract about the production of the anorexic body. While anorexics work individually on the creation of a reduced body mass, an extensive network of representational systems promotes the idea that for women to occupy less space with their bodies is desirable. However, the relationship between the individual reality of anorexia and the mass production of anorexia is complex and uncertain.

As I have argued elsewhere, the anorexic's language practice is similar to her spatial practice: in therapy she speaks, but often fills time with empty talk or talk about food rather than making connections between her unhappiness and her experiences. She measures time in terms of food: mealtimes, how long since she ate, what she will eat, how she will burn off the calories. Similarly she measures herself in contrast to others in terms of how much space they take up compared to her: are they bigger/smaller? She consciously positions her body so that she appears at her thinnest, especially in the presence of another thin person (Shipton, 1999).

What an anorexic cannot represent in language, she represents spatially, sometimes in the form of an absence (such as lack of menstrual periods, for example, which takes her decisively out of the reproductive category). Psychoanalytic theory enables us to think about the meanings for the individual of what is not verbalised. It may also be the case that there are larger, societal meanings, which follow the same track of non-articulation. Brennan (1993) argues that psychical processes are indeed acted out over time and geographical space, and proposes that this is rooted in our economic system. She presents several foundational phantasies about how we think about our being in the world. One is that we phantasise ourselves as active and the environment as passive and under our control. We also phantasise that we are energetically contained – we foreclose knowledge of connections between ourselves and other beings and entities. Western technology can fulfil some of the omnipotent desires expressed in these phantasies and so tends to encourage an acting out on a global scale that reinforces the power of the phantasy.

Turner compared anorexia to 'egoistic' suicide where an apparent individual, subjective to a choice to end life is also sociologically a result of the weakening of societal bonds and group membership, leaving the individual exposed to destructive forces of an individualistic culture (Durkheim, [1897] 1970). Anorexics seemed to be in the obverse situation of destroying themselves because of too much socialisation, control and surveillance in the family. Turner pointed out that, according to the literature he had read at the time, anorexics suffer from too much maternal control, with fathers being more distant or absent. He suggested that this undercuts the idea then that anorexia is linked to patriarchal values promoting and insisting upon thinness. However, he agreed with the feminist argument that anorexia is linked to women's position in general in society, but he suggested that it is not enough to locate the problem in the private space of the family since the wider industrial society determines what happens in individual households.

Sociologists and cultural theorists have commented on anorexia more than on any other eating disorder. This is partly because of the popular iconisation of the thin woman (see Malson, 1998), and because anorexia is amenable to many different readings. This arouses suspicion about the ease with which theory appears to decode what is going on. Yet, the extent of subclinical disorders in the female population (Hsu, 1990) indicates that many adult women are also preoccupied with their dietary practice and with regulating the volume of space their body takes up in the world. Each of those discourses on anorexia, bulimia and obesity constructs a different paradigm. Since problematised eating has itself become normative, and exhortations to manage body fat and diet are commonplace, a fundamental problem is created for psychological practitioners who wish to focus on a definite clinical phenomenon yet, at the same time, avoid pathologising women in general.

## Globalisation: views from mainstream clinicians

Many mainstream clinicians, most notably, Gordon (1990, 2000 and 2001) have drawn attention to a perceived increase in the number of countries reporting a growth in eating disorders. Although they take a less theorised approach to the question of the cultural dimensions of eating disorders, they make links to 'globalisation'. Gordon, for example, tells us:

> With the rapid industrialisation and urbanisation of large areas of the world previously isolated from Euro-American influence, and with the general globalisation of culture, associated with the ever-increasing influence of the mass media, a number of reports of an increasing prevalence of anorexia nervosa have appeared from areas previously considered relatively immune to such conditions. In particular, reports have emerged of an increased incidence of eating disorders in the Middle East, Africa, India and various countries in Southern Asia, including Hong Kong, China, Singapore, and South Korea. (Gordon, 2000: 80)

In this quotation we can see a range of processes hinted at as having some link with the development of anorexia, in particular: globalisation seems to include a host of processes, all rather complex and controversial. Van Esterik points out that modernisation should not be conflated with Westernisation. In Japan, for example, Western cultural practices in relation to food have not been adopted in a widespread way (Van Esterik, 2001: 20). But closer examination of the evidence given to support the argument that there is a spread of eating disorders occurring across the world, or as Gordon puts it 'a contemporary epidemic' (2000: 214), has not convinced everyone. One problem has been that many studies have taken surveys of attitudes to eating disorders as evidence that a diagnosed eating disorder exists (Palmer, 2001). Another problem Palmer notes is that there has been little epidemiological data collected in the past against which to compare more recent trends (ibid.).

Gordon replicated a previous study of Harvard students (Heatherton *et al.*, 1995) which found that the incidence of dieting, weight dissatisfaction and eating disorder symptoms had decreased since the 1980s (Gordon and Neal, 1998). This has led him to suppose that cultural influences such as feminism and anti-dieting education may have influenced the students to reject preoccupation with weight and dieting. Yet we are still unclear about what the relationship of self-reported attitudes and symptoms or dieting is to actual incidence. Others have queried whether there really has been an expansion of eating disorders such as anorexia in the UK (Fombonne, 1995). Making clear links between societal changes and the development of individual disorders is very hard, especially when researchers' trainings can bias them to perceiving phenomena in a particular light. The same material may have been viewed differently hitherto.

A very interesting case in point is the study of anorexia in Hong Kong by Lee (2001: 40–54). He points out that a fear of getting fat, though an important feature of the differential diagnosis in the *Diagnostic and Statistical Manual IV* (*DSM IV*) for anorexia was not a symptom he found when studying anorexics in Hong Kong. They had no fear of getting fat, a quality still linked to health in Chinese thinking, but were food refusers who expressed their worries or asserted themselves within their families in this way, not unlike Orbach described in *Hunger Strike* (1986). The use of *DSM*, a major framework for classifying psychiatric disorders, is particularly problematic, not only for eating disorders says Lee, but in relation to other major conditions such as depression. Lee says: 'According to its epistemological mandates, a psychiatric disorder has a pathognomic "core" that is rooted in some universal and presumably biological changes' (2001: 50). In depression a depressed mood is 'core' even though there is evidence that the condition is mediated by somatic experience in many parts of the world. Likewise, fat phobia is not universally present in anorexia in Hong Kong, nor is it always elsewhere or present all the time throughout anorexia. Just how exactly we are then to understand the classifications used in surveys and case studies becomes more complex.

Littlewood, commenting on Lee's work, makes links to dissociation and spirit possession as a response to loss of agency in some cultures:

We cannot presume that the final common pathway of self-starvation is reached in India, Hong Kong, Britain or elsewhere by

THE CULTURAL CONTEXT OF EATING DISORDERS

the identical antecedents, but at a high level of generality we might argue for analogous subjective and objective renunciations by women, a limited self-determination through extreme self-denial. And it is precisely in the ambiguous shift to 'modernity', with the loss of other instrumental strategies of personal resistance and with the ubiquity of potentially unlimited consumption, that these become heightened through the medicalised emphasis on a purified and self-sufficient body as the locus of personal agency. (Littlewood, 2001: 58)

Others, like Gordon, have also seen eating disorders as 'barometers of cultural change' (Rathner *et al.*, 1995; Nasser, 1997). Indeed, Rathner *et al.* were able to compare a study of eating attitudes carried out in Austria, Hungary, the Czech Republic and Poland before 1989 with one carried out in the mid-1990s. They found similar scores for the countries in transition after the reorganisation of post-Soviet Eastern Europe as were found for Western Europe. However, one fascinating finding was the emergence of dieting amongst men. Even so, what was monitored were attitudes and self reports, not cases of eating disorders, diagnosed according to accepted criteria (albeit contentious) by qualified practitioners. I want instinctively to agree with Rathner when he says that:

Globalisation might be the 21st century synonym for imperialism, that is, the concentration of economy and power on a previously unknown level. ... Globalisation is not an 'out there' phenomenon removed from the concerns of everyday life, but rather it is an 'in here' matter which affects or rather is dialectically related to even the most intimate aspects of our lives. (2001: 99)

However, Rathner does not offer us a way of demonstrating that what he asserts is true. I have tried to track some links in my clinical work (see Shipton, 1999), using a framework based on Lefebvre (1974). Yet, this detailed analysis of the opening phase of psychoanalytic psychotherapy with an anorexic young woman can only speculate about how we get globalisation 'in here', on the inside of our minds and, most importantly for me, how we can resist it. But here we need to reconsider the term globalisation because it risks losing any explanatory power since it has become such a plastic word. One definition of globalisation comes straight from the 'horse's mouth', (Joseph Stiglitz, the former Chief Economist at the World Bank and a Nobel Laureate in Economics in 2001):

> Fundamentally, it is the closer integration of the countries and peoples of the world which has been brought about by the enormous reduction of costs of transportation and communication, and the breaking down of artificial barriers to the flows of goods, services, capital, knowledge, and (to a lesser degree) people across borders. (Stiglitz, 2002: 9)

Stiglitz is disappointed in how globalisation has failed the poorer countries and that they have tended to be poorer as a result rather than richer – the flow of wealth has been back to the most wealthy capitalist countries. Lefebvre saw a cultural and representational network, which accompanied this process. It involves a world of commodities with worldwide strategies for making profits, and political structures to ensure this takes place, supported by a web of banks, manufacturing and business centres, transport networks and information channels. The dominant cultural imperative is to buy, and a whole plethora of representational systems work on us to make us feel we want to spend our money on what is offered to us. It is difficult to imagine how Stiglitz could believe globalisation would have anything other than a depressing affect on the economies of the developing world.

At best, we can say that there might be an association between media images of thinness and eating disorders. It has been argued that vulnerable women may be more inclined to take in such images as messages about how they should conform and develop an eating disorder, whereas most women only become dissatisfied with themselves and buy the products associated with thinness such as exercise machines, diets, slimming aids, cosmetic surgery, membership of gymnasia and so on. However, as Lee showed, the fear of fat is only one dimension of one kind of eating disorder: a particular kind of anorexia. A study carried out by Becker *et al.* (2002) in Fiji showed the impact on the teenage female population who had not previously seen TV when it had been introduced for three years. The girls wanted to be like the characters in the programmes and expressed dissatisfaction with the way they looked themselves. Crisp thought the consequences might be as follows:

> My own hunch is that Fijian females may not often be prone to the avoidance behaviours that probably underwrite anorexia nervosa. In the face of such Western influences, as Becker *et al* address,

paradoxically some of them instead may become the first generation of dyslipophobically obese in their homeland; more will be smitten with bulimia nervosa. (Crisp, 2002: 480–2)

The documented rise in obesity and bulimia (a definition, albeit a contested one, of obesity is given in Chapter 5) is also thought to be partly related to chaotic eating resultant on dieting and encouraged by media images of thinness (Polivy and Herman, 1985; Hsu, 1997). Palmer (2001) also points out that the commonest form of eating disorder may be classified as EDNOS (Eating Disorders Not Otherwise Specified) which throws into relief again the problem of classification. It may be that 'disordered' eating has become the norm.

There are many differences across cultures, 'Asian', for example covers some very different societies, as does the term 'East European': countries have very different histories, ethnicities, religions, gender relations and economies yet are often lumped together. What is also a puzzle is why women are being seen as more likely to be influenced by the media than are men. Those researchers like Gordon, Katzman and Nasser (2001) who argue that women adopt eating disorders at times of transition as a way of coping in an unstable world, need to find out how that happens to them and not so much to men. Gunew (2001: 168) has commented, on the way a discourse, which is really about beauty, has become coded as one about health. All in all, we need much more particular understanding than we presently possess. Just as we no longer deem the fasting and starving girls of thirteenth-century saintly history as being the same as contemporary anorexics, similarly we should be aware that self-starvation, eating and then vomiting, and obesity, may mean different things to different people at different times, or indeed, to one person at different times. This is not the stuff of sexy media headlines, but is the reality of truly trying to make sense of what happens individually and culturally. We need an exchange of ideas between different disciplines to help produce knowledge that can honour the complexities involved in thinking about any links between culture and eating disorders. The issues are complex and we will return to them in Chapter 7.

Some key points

- There is no universal, ahistorical 'normal' body.
- There is no universal, ahistorical 'normal' eating.
- Dissatisfaction with body size and shape is common and may be linked with the spread of Western images of particular iconic figures.
- There is a commercial interest at work in promoting self-improvement and body-improvement.
- Whether or not there is an increase in eating disorders is debatable.
- Classifications are themselves not necessarily universally applicable.
- The relationship between culture and individual psyche is complex and intriguing.
- Most people do not develop an eating disorder though they may be involved with diets and body practices.

# 3

# ANOREXIA NERVOSA

Anorexia nervosa is described in the ICD 10 (International Statistical Classification of Diseases and Related Health Problems [10th Revision]) Classification of Mental and Behavioural Disorders as: '...deliberate weight loss, induced and/or sustained by the patient' (WHO, 1992). For a definite diagnosis, all the following are required:

- Body weight is maintained at least 15 per cent below that expected either because it has been lost or never achieved.
- Weight loss is achieved by avoiding fattening foods. One or more of the following self-induced strategies should be present: vomiting; purging; excessive exercise; use of appetite suppressants and/or diuretics.
- There is a body-image distortion with a dread of fatness experienced as an intrusive overvalued idea with resulting self-imposed low weight.
- There is endocrinal disorder leading to amenorrhoea in women and loss of potency or sexual interest in men. There may be elevated levels of growth hormone and cortisol, changes in thyroid hormone and abnormalities of insulin secretion.
- If onset is before puberty, development is delayed or arrested and growth ceases so that girls do not develop breasts and there is primary amenorrhoea, and in boys the genitals remain juvenile. With recovery, puberty is often completed normally but girls may have their first period delayed.

Some physical results of anorexia are coldness, rough, dry skin, sometimes fluid retention in the ankles or face, loss of hair on the head and a fine down-like growth of hair on the body (lanugo). Emaciation causes the muscles to waste away and there is a risk of osteoporosis in later life if emaciation has been for a long period. There may be a fast heart rate and sleep is disrupted.

The diagnostic criteria for anorexia show how anorexia and bulimia are closely related, with only the overeating bouts as a clear distinguishing factor in bulimia. This feature of classification and the emergence of bulimia as a distinct entity, long after anorexia was described, means that the literature on anorexia is often really about both anorexia and bulimia. Where possible, for the purposes of this book I have tried to tease them apart. To my mind there is a distinction between never taking in enough food, on the one hand, and taking it in, but not being able keep it inside and trying to get rid of it, on the other. Some people have used the terms 'restrictor anorexic' for one group and 'bulimic anorexic' for the other (Farrell, 1995). It is difficult to pinpoint what it is that is different but, in psychotherapy, it seems to me that it is much harder to help put someone restricting intake, in touch with their real feelings. The distinctions, though are not clear, and as all practitioners know, the same individual may start out anorexic and end up bulimic. For the purposes of this chapter I will try to focus on the restrictor anorexic but am sure, in advance, that it will not be altogether possible to find literature that refers solely to such people. Furthermore, I am of the opinion that when we look under the surface of any eating disorder, there is a constellation of common issues, though I do not quite subscribe to the 'continuum of eating disorders' idea, as it flattens out a complex interacting set of issues and defences.

The whole area of eating disorders has been researched and written about extensively, in the last 40 years, in particular by Hilde Bruch in the USA and Arthur Crisp and Christopher Fairburn in the UK, and hundreds of others across the world. Gordon believes that some 700 publications each year on eating disorders appear in professional journals alone (Gordon, 2000: vi). The psychoanalytic literature is formidable in size and the rough guide to it below must remain far from comprehensive. However I want to go back to the earliest psychoanalytic writing on anorexia, since it is the base from which Bruch, in particular, started and later reacted against, and it contains many rich ideas which may have some worth for practitioners today.

## Early psychoanalytic contributions to understanding anorexia

Anorexia was a symptom in several hysterical patients whose treatment concerned Freud. One such was Breuer's patient, Anna O, who gave up eating and would only accept food from the hand of her doctor, at one stage. Another was Frau Emmy Von N., a patient Freud treated who recoiled in disgust from eating. Both of these patients were also prone to dramatic and bizarre symptoms in line with the diagnosis of conversion hysteria formulated by Freud. In Studies on Hysteria (1893–95), Freud pointed out that symptoms can change and that they are usually overdetermined; many different factors influence their formation, and they can be understood in different ways, at different times. However, at this early stage in the development of psychoanalysis, Freud's emphasis was on the way a refusal to eat, or a feeling of disgust when tasting food, might indicate a psychosexual fixation at the oral stage of development. He saw such symptoms generally as combining an unconscious wish for something illicit and a defence against it – a basic tenet of the psychoanalytic approach which still offends many people. In Freud's analysis of Dora (1905) he found that she had turned away from food after her encounter with the intrusive attentions of Herr K, although he believed she was aroused by the man. Freud also linked anorexia to melancholia in an early paper of 1895 (Birksted-Breen, 1989).

Another tenet is that one zone of satisfaction can be used to satisfy a wish that would normally be satisfied elsewhere, so that mouth and vagina can be substituted for each other in unconscious phantasy, as can anus and mouth, and anus and vagina. This has meant that many early views of anorexia, and of course myriad other difficulties, have been linked with sexual impulses, and in women, fear of being made pregnant. The basic premise was that there could be a fear of being impregnated through the mouth so food intake was curtailed. A fear may also be accompanied by an overwhelming wish for what is feared. Similar views have been evinced since (e.g. Waller, Kaufman and Deutsch, 1940; Thomä, 1967). Berlin et al. (1951) also mentioned oral sadistic wishes as well as reaction formation against incorporative wishes. Falstein et al. (1956) found a different, though linked, dynamic in a male anorexic who wished to get rid of fat in order to get rid of a feminine identification.

Meyer and Weinroth (1957) perceived the anorexic as attempting to restore the mother–child bond. Jessner and Abse (1960) wrote about oral deprivation by the mother followed by gratification and closeness. The resulting ambivalence, which would undermine the maturation of the girl in all the phases that followed on, leads to a tendency to regress back to the oral/anal stage under stress. Since the 1960s, in the USA at least, the emphasis shifted from constitutional problems to object relations, separation–individuation and the development of a fully functioning, gendered self. Sours found a wide spectrum of psychopathology and developmental deficiency (1969) and was one of the first to distinguish between different groups of anorexics: those who could be treated with ordinary psychoanalytic therapy and those more disturbed people for whom the approach had to be modified, and who may need auxiliary medical management (1974). Sours tells us that over time analysts went beyond impregnation fantasies to a more pluralist understanding. He himself has focussed on the effects of the mother's narcissistic use of her child (Sours, 1980). Schwartz (1988) thought the anorexic, by becoming so thin and phallic looking, was unconsciously turning herself into a penis and, in phantasy, displacing father in order to take his place.

Some clinicians have moved too from an emphasis on the individual anorexic's developmental deficits to the anorexic family (Selvini-Palazzoli, 1974), along with a shift from splitting processes within the anorexic psyche to a more systemic approach in family therapy.

One of the most influential clinicians in the USA is Hilde Bruch. She has researched and written extensively on eating disorders. She moved away from a classical Freudian understanding to one that emphasises how the anorexic has developed a faulty way of interpreting her own needs and internal states, as a result of deficiencies in mothering. Bruch identified three areas in which an anorexic is troubled: body image, perception and a sense of effectiveness (1966, 1970), and described how the pursuit of thinness is a kind of defective solution to her problems. Bruch came to see some forms of anorexia as closely related to the developmental patterns she perceived in schizophrenia, though the quest for autonomy and effectiveness through control of the body distinguished anorexia.

Bruch came to the conclusion that the normal interpretative way of carrying out psychoanalytic therapy was too depriving and ineffectual in the treatment of anorexics and moved towards a more supportive form of psychotherapy. Swift argued that she interpreted more than she thought that she did (1991: 53). More discussion of the implications of Bruch's work for technique is found in Chapter 6.

In the USA, a considerable influence on clinical work with people with eating disorders has come from the field of self-psychology. Eating disorders are understood as disorders of the self, where there has been a traumatic, long-term disturbance in the empathic connection between parents and child. The failure of parenting means the child does not internalise self-soothing and tension-regulating structures, and later in life tries to substitute for the lack by way of anorexic and bulimic behaviour. A danger to the self and an effort at

restoring it are re-enacted. Food is used as an archaic self-object.*
In this view

> ... anorexia and bulimia represent neither unconscious com-
> promises, symbolically acted out control battles with parents, nor
> internalised societal preoccupations with thinness; rather, they
> actualise life and death struggles to maintain the integrity of the
> self and prevent disintegration anxiety. (Geist, 1989: 25)

Birksted-Breen (1989) discussed the anorexic's fear of, and wish
for, fusion with her mother and found others had commented on it
too: Bruch (1973); Boris (1984a, b); Sprince (1984); Hughes *et al.* (1985);
Sprince (1988) and Birksted-Breen (1989) emphasise the problem the
anorexic has as a result of a deprivation or lack of a transitional space
in which to develop the capacity to symbolise. They demonstrate that
psychoanalytic work involves creating a transitional space. In the
USA, the influence of Mahler's work on merger and the individuation–
separation phase has affected much of the work on eating disorders
but has had less impact on British psychoanalytic thinking, influenced as it is by the work of Klein, and the infant observational
method developed by Bick. It is to a more object relational view of
anorexia, influenced by Klein and Bion that I now want to turn to,
especially the idea of anorexia and bulimia being linked to a frightening, voracious appetite for the object.

## Anorexia as a defence against bulimic desires

How anorexia develops as a defence against bulimia was elaborated
by Sohn (1985); Birksted-Breen (1989); Rey (1994). Anorexia is perceived by these analysts to be a response to a longing to feed greedily
initially, at the breast, overwhelming the individual who then sets up
controls around food and eating to prevent what is felt as a potential
catastrophe. As Ellen West, a famous and tragic anorexic patient of
Binswanger, wrote: 'I don't think the dread of becoming fat is the
real ... neurosis but the constant desire for food' (quoted in Bordo,
1993b: 146).
    Klein (1952) suggested that babies feed in ways which can reflect
pressure from internal driving forces: devouring the contents of the

* The concept of self-object was developed by American analysts such as
Kohut and Stolorow. It has been described as a set of psychological functions
felt as necessary for self-experience (Stolorow *et al.*, 1987).

breast and fearing retaliation when they are under the sway of destructive feelings. As, for example, when they have been kept waiting and hungry to long. Or they can feed in a calmer, more satisfying way when they are content or have been responded to in a manner that counteracts anxiety and distress. Rey considered why feeding should feel so catastrophic to the anorexic, illustrating his ideas with the published autobiographical account of an anorexic's illness (Rouah, 1980 cited in Rey, 1994). Rey suggested that one terrifying phantasy about feeding might be that it means feeding off the body of the mother. In the case of the anorexic in question there was also a reversal phantasy whereby the mother was felt to be feeding off the body of the foetus. What was once true – we do feed from the maternal body through the placenta and later the breast – had become a dominant, enduring phantasy. In the primitive defence mechanisms of the mind of the infant (Klein, 1952), this idea is complemented by the persecutory notion that mother must wish to feed equally voraciously off the baby. Rey suggested the anorexic wishes to avoid this catastrophe by doing away with eating, though she cannot do away with her desire to eat.

The confusion about who is doing what to whom may be at the heart of the anorexic's thinking about herself and may affect her capacity to separate off from a mother who could then be conceived of as an individual with her own body and identity. In the normal development of a sense of self, the mother or caretaker assists the infant by literally and metaphorically holding and handling the infant in such a way that the relationship between inner and outer is mediated by a supporting and containing 'other' (Winnicott, 1960).

## 'Second-skin' function

Bick (1968) described the infant's experience of the skin in early object relations when the nascent personality cannot cohere on its own and relies on an external wrapping: the skin, for example. This function is supported by the holding activity of the mother who lends to the skin its emotion holding quality. As she offers the nipple from which to feed: her breast, her smell, her touch and voice become focal points around which the baby self coalesces. Later this capacity to enfold and contain becomes part of the personality itself giving the infant a sense of an inside which is contained, a self that contains and an outside which is contingent. In order for introjection, or taking in of a good experience with an object (modelled on the process of incorporation of food) to occur, space needs to have been made. Without it Bick says the infant must project everything outwards, hopefully into the mother's mind and her body where containment via projective identification can take place. An unsupported baby might seek a bright light or a sound as an alternative when satisfactory experience of a maternal container is lacking. A second skin is formed through which the infant holds herself together: this may be via mental or physical functions such as muscular self-holding where physical activity provides substitute holding by another and pseudo-independence. An infant who has not felt held together and who has not developed the capacity to contain will feel overwhelmed when faced with powerful forces which threaten her precarious equilibrium – strong feelings of all kinds will pose such a danger. Hunger and greed will not be experienced as transient states but as threats to be defended against. Talking and intellectualising can also become 'second-skin' containing activities. The anorexic seems to have made the exercise of her own willpower function as a 'second-skin', giving her a spurious sense of security through self-control and self-holding. Any help offered to the anorexic feels like an interference with her self-management and can be experienced by her as intrusive (Williams, 1997; Lawrence, 2002). However, Lawrence considers that the origin of this anxiety about intrusion springs from the anorexic's own wish to intrude upon and control others.

## Dimensionality

Meltzer (1975) further developed the idea of a 'second-skin' function to include dimensionality: without adequate three-dimensional containers we are unable to function in the world in a fully human and civilised way. His geography of mental space includes:

- inside the self
- outside the self
- inside internal objects
- inside external objects
- a fifth dimension of 'nowhere' beyond the gravitational pull of objects (as for example, in the states of mind of people who are deluded).

In the earliest stages of life a move away from one thing represents a move towards another: time being indistinguishable from distance. Gratification and fusion with the object are undifferentiated. Events are not retained for thought. This is one-dimensionality or mindless-ness. If memory cannot be contained, thought as trial action cannot take place. In two-dimensionality there is at least a skin-deep surface though the individual would be shallow (a 'paper-thin' personality). Only with containment can a self which is containing take shape. To develop this containing capacity we need to have been held and contained ourselves. We all need an 'other' who helps us produce this space within ourselves.

The mechanism we use in infancy to relate to other objects in space is projective identification: trying to get others to deal with our feel-ings for us. Adhesive identification is a version of identification in that the individual's whole sense of identity is held together by being projected onto another: taking up their shape like cling-film. To progress beyond this stage, we need to introject back into ourselves something with which we can identify more deeply and which we can hold within as an integrating nucleus. Identification with popu-lar icons of femininity may be fleeting and superficial for most young women, but for those without an internal space which can support the development of an identity of their own such identification may be adhesive. A young woman who rejects identification with her mother may be prone to such adhesions.

## Clinical illustrations

The state of mind whereby there is no internal space into which an anorexic can neither take good experience nor the sense of an external object onto or into which she can adequately project, has been likened to a 'no-entry' syndrome (Williams, 1997). Someone in this state of mind finds starting psychotherapy very difficult. The therapist struggles to make helpful interpretations but finds her own capacity for thinking is reduced (see Birksted-Breen, 1989). Psycho-analytic theory about the formation of inner dimensionality (space for thought), allied with attention to the more literal use of space by the anorexic, helps elucidate the beginning stage of therapy. This is especially useful when the anorexic is seeking to avoid giving up the solution to her unconscious dilemma and when there seems to be no point of entry for therapeutic input.

## Jenny: the psychotherapy of an anorexic

Jenny was a thin, pretty, 23-year-old speech therapist, with rather chapped looking hands and face. She was dressed very neatly and modestly as if going for a job interview. She had become anorexic at 18, in her gap year, when she had gone to work in a hospital in a distant city. There, she lodged with a lively young couple who enjoyed a relaxed life-style based around socialising, eating and drinking. In contrast, her family was abstemious, reserved and very career-minded. She returned home after eight months to find she had put on weight and that her sister had lost weight in her absence. Jenny stopped eating family meals, then began to diet and to exercise until she was thinner than her little sister. When she went off to university she became even thinner and depressed, and contemplated suicide by jumping through a window. She had been put on antidepressants by her General Physician (GP) and had seen a counsellor for a year. She had also met a young man who was studying psychology who seemed quite a support to her though he had some problems of his own. She had managed to graduate with a good degree.

Jenny's weight had stabilised but she wasn't menstruating and she was jogging most days. Nevertheless, she could hold down her new job, was in a relationship and had established a rather restricted food regimen which just about sustained her. This precarious balance was threatened by graduating, moving to another region, starting work and contemplating possibly moving in with her boyfriend, who was transferring to the same area soon. Recently, Jenny found herself cutting down on food like she had when she had originally started to lose weight. She did not want to become so ill again and had found a sympathetic GP who believed psychotherapy was what she needed and who put her back on antidepressants and made a referral to me.

Jenny's account of herself at assessment was as if from a psychology textbook. Unlike most anorexics, she was somewhat critical of her parents. She gave me a thumbnail sketch of the aetiology of her anorexia and her treatments, including counselling, which had made it all so clear to her, she said. She knew what was wrong, but it didn't seem to be helping her stop cutting down on food, she told me. I mainly listened and wondered what I could say that would add anything to this very insightful exposition. (Assessment for psychotherapy of eating disordered patients will be discussed further in Chapter 6.) Jenny was eloquent and courteous though rather formal. The only connection I was able to make to her was when she was telling me about the food she ate – as I was trying to understand whether she ate a normal slice of bread or a small one, I found myself adding 'ish?' on the end of her description of the size of a slice of bread as 'standard'.

She picked up on this and used the suffix herself several times, as I did. It felt very much as if my understanding of her and her acceptance of it was going to be measured out in very small quantities, as Williams says 'in coffeespoons' (1997). I also heard about how she would grind her teeth to such an extent that she had damaged them and noted the contrast between the beautiful language and measured tones and the anxious person who produced them.

When Jenny came back the next week to complete her assessment, she was upset. She said she went away the previous week and wondered what on earth she had been doing – she felt she had been trying to convince me she was alright and she wasn't. She didn't want to be on antidepressants for the rest of her life and she didn't want to get on a downward spiral with her eating. She told me more about her childhood and how she had once had a good relationship with her father and now it was awful. She got on better with her mother. She knew that her mother had been depressed when she was born and that she had been looked after mainly by her father. They had sent her to a school which she had hated, and were ambitious on her behalf because they themselves had underachieved. They were sorely disappointed that she hadn't trained as a doctor and were pleased that her younger sister was doing just that.

I will describe the three phases of Jenny's therapy, although they are not of equal length. I want to dwell more on the opening phase, as this is when it is a struggle to engage anorexic patients. This has led some commentators like Bruch (1970) to believe that a psychoanalytic intervention is to be avoided. The first phase of creating a space for Jenny to think about how she felt lasted about eight or nine months, though in some ways it remained a central issue. The second phase was longer: about a year and a half, and involved unpackaging her feelings, again, an ongoing issue. The last phase was working towards an ending. The therapy lasted three years and was terminated because Jenny felt she had improved enough to 'go it alone' and was struggling to pay for her therapy without the financial assistance that her parents had originally given her, and which had come to an end after a year. While she was greatly improved in terms of well-being and physical health at this point, she and I both agreed that there was a lot more work to do at a deeper level. I would count Jenny's therapy as successful all the same, but far from complete. In an ideal world I would have liked to offer Jenny a more intense experience, perhaps three times a week or more, after the first few years. However, once-a-week therapy was all that she could cope with in the beginning, and that seemed adequate at the time.

## First phase: creating a space for an emotional experience

To enter into the psychotherapy clinic where she had once a week early morning sessions before work, Jenny needed to knock at the door as it was still locked until the receptionist arrived a little later. The first time Jenny arrived she rang the doorbell which sounded very faintly in the locked reception area. When the first interview with her was finished I explained how she must knock at the door to make herself heard in the future.

The next week, however, she rang the bell. This went on until I realised that Jenny's inability to go directly for what she needed was not accidental: it reflected an indirect and controlling relationship to her object. Jenny had been a premature baby who was kept in an incubator for weeks before going home to a mother who was afraid to hold her and anxious about mothering. Jenny had thrived in hospital and had been described as a real 'toughie' despite being a very small baby: this lusty description embarrassed her. Jenny managed to get what she wanted but not by simply latching directly onto the nipple as it were, or putting her fist to the door. On one occasion she had been looking through the glass door at me while ringing the bell – I heard nothing so was oblivious. There seemed to be a phantasy here that if she could see me I could see her as if there were no separation or different perspective. Similarly, she was in a constant dilemma about knowing how much to eat and looked to everyone to find out how much they ate. She had no internal sense of 'enough'.

Jenny kept me in her sight, though on occasion was able to tolerate me looking away or not meeting her gaze. I was nevertheless surprised when I realised on a day when thick snow had begun to fall outside my window that, as she appeared to look out of the window of the room (a new event about which I made an erroneous interpretation), she had not really looked out at all. In fact, she had turned her head in a simulation of looking away from me, imitating my reaction to the blizzard, and had not noticed the snow. Jenny was imitating my movements like an infant follows the mother's lead in relating to space outside the nursing couple.

Jenny always sat on the edge of her chair with no support for her back and looking physically uncomfortable. She held herself together in a tense and restricted way, using her muscularity even in apparent repose. Returning after a break in which she seemed to thrive, I suggested to Jenny that she might feel relieved that she had been able do without me and her therapy. The session went quite well and for the first time (six months into her therapy) I began to feel as if I could attune myself to her thoughts as she talked about feeling painfully alone. I found myself picturing a suicide scenario that she had once described and had ruminated about when she was younger. She then went on to talk about the very same scene and how close she came to carrying out her plan of jumping through a window. I had tuned in correctly. After this session Jenny missed her appointment – as if she felt my understanding her as a narcissistic wound to her own invulnerability. She could not tolerate me thinking what she had not yet thought. Perhaps she also needed to make sure that she really could do without me.

After the missed session Jenny returned and for the first time ever, she sat back in the chair looking almost relaxed and expansive. My understanding of the meaning of her behaviour in this session was not based on her use of space alone, but both the missing of the session and her temporary ease on return encouraged me to believe I had been right in the previous session (too right – she had needed to put me in my place!). Missing a session had made her feel tri-umphantly back in control of her self and of the process of her therapy. When I put this interpretation to Jenny as tactfully as I could she visibly relaxed further.

Leaving the therapeutic space was also full of tension. I ended the session on time each week and Jenny would sit and look at me. I had to make a gesture as if about to get up before she would stir. Sometimes I had to stand up and walk towards the door. I couldn't draw her attention to what this might mean as it was happening – there was no time left. Jenny always began the sessions rapidly, bringing a lot of material I think she had already thought about so that it became difficult to comment on both her arriving and her departing: boundaries she wished to control. Therapeutic space was hard to establish: the way it opened up and closed remained a prob-lem for some time, as if starting and finishing were like bodily sphincter-functions that had to be kept under careful control.

The use of language to avoid the communication of affects is exceptionally marked in anorexia. As Modell commented in relation to patients who do not communicate effectively, the analyst feels she 'is drowning in a sea of words ' (Modell, 1980: 259). Although anorex-ics, who usually feel very lonely and misunderstood, go into therapy in order to have someone to whom they can relate and hopefully who will be able to understand how they feel, their initial use of words manages to produce talk but fails to produce emotional meaning.

Jenny's talk was eloquent and she loved to use 'le mot juste'. Her thoughts were apparently logical, precise, coherent and fast moving. As I finished my sentences, Jenny would be agreeing with me, corroborating my interpretation, even before she had fully heard it, let alone thought about it. She appropriated my comments, adhered to them and finished them off herself. There was no 'space' for thought. Indeed, Jenny has said she was unable to know what she thought or felt about another person in their presence – she could only know such things in their absence. In other words, she needed an internal space in which to think and could not at first sustain the space in my presence, as if she and I were not separate when together.

In Jenny's talk in her early sessions I never knew who was who: friends had no names when she talked about them, anecdotes were vague and unspecific. Scenes were described about which she gave no concrete details. In a bulimic relation to an object the individual cares little about the quality of relationship but is driven by a desire to have the object. All objects thus become interchangeable because the urge to satisfy a desire is the overriding aspect. Jenny worked very hard and would develop her own insights into situations usually without my help: her explanations would be intellectually convincing and often elaborate but devoid of emotional depth. Jenny's insights did not nurture a sense of well being in her, either. Food is the substance from which everything is made at the beginning of life and in therapy words represent a similar substance. Anorexic patients like Jenny do not starve the therapist of words but strip them of their emotional meanings and specificity. The content of their discourse seems less significant than its effect. The lack of a rewarding relationship to a specific object becomes hidden beneath an apparent attachment to many unsatisfying objects and the anorexic's speech similarly loses its particular and varied emotional inflections.

In me, there was a complementary pull to provide quick fast food which was not nutritional, not specific to Jenny. I found myself grabbing one idea after another like a bulimic-therapist. My function to provide specific interpretation designed to address her particular needs felt under attack: my thinking and my words didn't help. As Jenny moved into a phase of beginning to symbolise emotional experience she did so by making gestures and adding words to them, much as a baby learns to speak. For example, she explained how my comments in an earlier session had really hit her and illustrated this by tapping herself in the chest which made a resounding noise. She went on to talk about a fear of emptiness inside in connection with this echoing noise as if she was really only just finding a separate, three-dimensional self and emotional words to go with it.

Normally, there should be no interruptions to a therapeutic session and when they do occur they are usually very distressing to both patient and therapist. In Jenny's case, unfortunately an interruption did occur. We were disrupted by a very loud noise in the corridor and someone knocking at the door but this made no difference to Jenny and did not make much impact on me either. The phantasy behind this was that we were not two people meeting: I must be a part of her or she must be a part of me. We couldn't be interrupted.

After the first planned holiday break our session had to be unavoidably cancelled. I rang Jenny very early in the day to let her know before she set off for the clinic. At her next session she described the phone call as interrupting a dream in which she was trying to feed her mother. In the dream she thought how difficult it was when someone would not eat the food you gave them: mother wanted only certain foods not others. As she woke from the dream she wanted to report it to me as a 'breakthrough' and was looking forward to seeing me after her first break. She answered my phone call and then went back to sleep. She woke later, not knowing whether she had dreamed me phoning or not. Jenny was upset about this interruption, as well as feeling disappointed at the cancellation, she felt as if I had punctured her dream-space, where she and I were all mixed up like a mother and daughter, with daughter still inside mother's womb feeding and at the same time trying to give something back to feed mother.

## Middle phase: unpackaging feelings

As we continued to meet it became more and more possible for a process of exploration to open up Jenny's tightly controlled inner world and for experiences which touched her to be allowed some expression. Jenny's feelings of jealousy towards her sister began to erupt – she felt absolutely betrayed by me in one session when I tried to understand something she said about her, as if I was more inter-ested in her than in Jenny. She felt devastated at the extent to which she could not bear being the only one in her mother's mind, and mine. Her wish to be able to control how her boyfriend thought also came to the fore. She started to feel anger and expressed her feelings directly to people who upset her but then would retreat to 'dry' ground by distancing herself through intellectualising, leaving far more primitive feelings of rage less disturbed. However, a process had begun and Jenny began to express her sadness too, at the lack of understanding between her and her mother. Jenny thought that she was 'too much' for anyone else to understand and had always thought she had to depend on herself to understand. There was an ebb and flow of openness to her feelings and then a reaction against loss of control. Sometimes the language Jenny used suggested there was a threat of liquefaction if she didn't keep a strict control on herself internally – she often talked about being afraid of being 'wet' or that she felt 'wishy-washy'. She described how her mother was unable to bathe her when she was a small child – she refused to sit in the bath and let the water rise up over her. At other times, when I was able to make an emotional contact with Jenny, she felt this almost physically, telling me that she felt I had made 'indentations' in her 'shell' and she would often react in the period between sessions against what felt like being 'prodded' by me. I think that my words were experienced very concretely.

As Jenny became more in touch with some of her wishes and fears, she also allowed herself to taste more kinds of food – even eating cheese. She began to slowly put on weight and her periods came back. She became afraid of getting greedy. Sometimes she was greedy for my thoughts and asked me direct questions which felt intrusive, as if she wanted to get something out of me before it had formed. I mentioned this to her and she linked it to how she would also complete peoples' sentences, just like her father did. Her father came into her thoughts much more than he had before, and she seemed to have established a better relationship with him but her relationship with her mother had worsened. She told me a dream in which the vicar had come to her old school and had the task of impregnating all the girls. Her father intervened, in what seemed like a protective way, and insisted that he, himself, should be the one to impregnate his daughter. This seemed 'OK' to her in the dream. She was quite puzzled by the dream and I tentatively offered an interpretation about her wish to be close to her father, to be daddy's little girl and to have him to herself, like her mother did and have his baby. This brought back to her mind a memory of father putting mother under his umbrella and leaving out her and her sister. Yet she remembered feeling pleased about this and that it was right and proper. I thought she was relieved that mother really did have father – she may have a wish to take him away but if she succeeded it would be dreadful. This led on to her saying that she also felt betrayed by mother who was herself very possessive, and had been jealous of Jenny's wish to be with her boyfriend rather than with her one summer. Who was jealous or envious of whom became a theme that was played out at work and in the transference with me.

Jenny began to enjoy more in life than working and running and began to pick up some of her old interest in singing, and joined an operatic group. After much agonising she decided to share a house with her boyfriend and got very involved in renovating it. She began to think about having a baby. At this point, she expressed some very long-standing fears about what she may have done to the inside of her body by starving, though her anxiety about whether or not she could have a baby went back to early childhood. It was as if she felt she was very damaged deep down inside. This may have also been related to a phantasy that she had damaged mother's insides too. Another aspect of this fear is how it related to Jenny's sense of self. Jenny had always dreaded people asking her what she thought when she was quiet because she really didn't know, and one boyfriend had ditched her because she never had anything to say. In the past, she had hated people talking about what she was like 'deep down' because she hadn't believed there was anything at all deep down inside her.

## Final phase: coming to an end

As Jenny's career became established and her relationship with her boyfriend moved more in the direction of marriage, Jenny started to wonder about whether she could afford to terminate her therapy. She was now the main breadwinner as her boyfriend had decided to study for a PhD. She was afraid of lapsing into a downward spiral of cutting back on food when stressed, but she hadn't so far actually got any thinner than she was when I met her and had put on weight. I didn't know how much – this was between her and her GP whom she had seen originally every few weeks to be weighed but the GP stopped asking her back after seeing that she was not losing weight. There was a period of several months when we explored what this wish to end was about and it seemed ambiguous. However, Jenny decided she wanted to try to see if she could manage without me, although she wanted reassurance she could come back into therapy in the future. It was hard to get Jenny to face the fact that ending would involve a loss and that she might feel bereft. At our last meeting, she told of how much her parents had not wanted her to stay in therapy once she was no longer at risk. She was angry with her parents' inability to face their own feelings and critical of the way they compartmentalised emotions. The parallels with her predicament were all too obvious. When the session came to an end, she sat for a few minutes, seeming not to want to leave and I felt I had been mistaken to agree to ending (not that I could stop her). Sprince has commented on how the therapist has to 'come to terms with limited achievements which may include precipitate terminations or marriages' (1988: 87) and warns that in some cases a partner may serve as a receptacle for aspects of the anorexic self. I hope this was not the case for Jenny. Boris (1984) also warns that the anorexia solution to passionate desires can always be returned to and that the anorexic may only appear to give up her solution in favour of the clinician's solution. He believes it is for this reason that some short-term interventions in behaviour therapy and family therapy appear to be successful.

Jenny's was not the most severe example of anorexia one can meet but her case is rather typical of the sort of work that can go on in outpatient clinics, student counselling services, private practice, voluntary agencies, low-fee clinics and maybe still some GP practices, when the patient is seen for once- or twice-a-week therapy by a psychotherapist, psychodynamic counsellor or clinical psychologist of a psychoanalytic orientation.

## When therapy breaks down

I want to briefly mention two other anorexics to give some thought to the range of difficulties that can be encountered in anorexia. I would like to discuss some of the anorexics I met in psychiatric in-patient units but lack of hospital notes makes it so difficult to talk in anything other than generalities. My experience was that real psychotherapeutic work did not begin until they were out-patients: there was such little mental space for psychological thinking when patients were at a very low weight. However, it was often my role, especially when I was a student occupational therapist, to simply talk to patients in order to understand their illness. It was by sitting and talking that I discovered why one young woman was losing weight despite being watched as she ate three meals a day. She would be sick in the sink, would exercise all the time and drink nothing but black coffee. It seems unbelievable now but at the time no one had realised she did this. Another young woman deteriorated dramatically when she was brought into hospital, stopped eating altogether, took to her bed, stopped getting up to go to the toilet and became incontinent, deluded and eventually became mute. My opinion has always been that hospital is a last resort option for people with eating disorders. An eating-disordered patient can completely dominate a ward, splitting the medical team and can become absolutely gripped by a destructive part of the personality that wants to push him or her and the staff to the limit.

The next patient I want to talk about was a student: Peta. She had been referred by her GP who also sent her to a psychiatrist. I saw her for ten months but this period was interrupted by holidays, non-attendance and field trips, so in a way, it was a brief encounter. Peta was a twin, in her second year at university, and anorexic since she was 16. She and her sister had started dieting together but her sister gave up, leaving Peta to outdo her on this front (and on no other). Peta was small in height and weighed five stone when I met her. She was always dressed in baggy, drab clothes. She had short, unruly hair, was pale, with sunken cheeks and she sometimes gave off an unpleasant smell. However, there was something about her that was rather charming. At first she would turn up with a large rucksack on her back, full of weighty tomes. She told me that she was 'the runt of the litter'. All her siblings (four others) had done better than her at school. She missed her twin and didn't fit in anywhere. She was living on a very small amount of money and as she talked excitedly, seemed quite manic and out of touch with her feelings. I tried to establish rapport with her but it was hard going. She would only look at me out of the corner of her eye and give me very suspicious looks. She had been threatened with admission to hospital if she didn't put on any weight and I presumed she was complying with seeing me as part of a strategy of keeping out of hospital. Over the next seven months she put on two pounds.

Seeing Peta was delicate work: she was at times, evasive and at times, forthcoming. I tried to say what I thought was happening but to little avail. I talked to my clinical supervisor about her and how she smelled and how, sometimes, odd though it sounds, she looked as if she had a cushion shoved up her jumper. His advice was that I should comment on it, but I was reluctant. We both wondered if she was vomiting or purging and if that might explain why she smelled. We did not know what the bulge under her jumper implied. It certainly made her look pregnant. I did mention, as tactfully as I could, that she seemed to be neglecting herself and I wondered why that was so. This led to an account of how tidy and orderly her mother was and the arguments she had always got into over her appearance and her messiness. Unsolicited, she volunteered that she thought she might be smelly because she was sweating such a lot at the moment, though she was having a bath every day, she insisted. She would not accept anything remotely interpretative from me and seemed to want to keep me idealised. My comments made a slight difference – she stopped smelling, and the cushion didn't appear anymore, if that is what it was.

Peta talked about food and about her studies. She had one friend on whom she had become very dependent and who seemed like a twin substitute. She chatted to me in a way that made it difficult to find a point of entry into her emotional life. As an example of this, during one session she skipped between talking about how lonely she felt, how fascinated she was by her academic subject, how she struggled to keep up with the coursework, though she had good practical skills (she was studying landscape architecture) and, bizarrely, how she had been invited to an Ann Summers party where she thought there would be sex aids to try out. Peta was a virgin, and hated sexual innuendo. Her discourse was often a similar odd mix that felt like a sickly confection, and made me feel dizzy and disorientated. Over the weeks she brought me a collection of her poems, which were well written. Re-reading them today, I am still surprised at just how good they are. Unbidden, she said I could use them in anything I ever wrote about anorexia. I felt I could not reach her and that she was out of touch with herself.

Peta looked back longingly to an apparently idyllic childhood. The family moved house when she was 11 and she started a new school where she was unhappy. She had been a tomboy and harboured dreams of being able to live close to nature in what she called a 'tribal' way. She clearly felt a regressive pull back in time to an earlier her, but what this really entailed was not possible to discover. Over time, despite the superficiality of the work, there were some changes. She stopped bringing her mound of books and seemed slightly less anxious, although she still looked like a scarecrow. She was very angry with me because I would not side with her against her GP who was monitoring her weight regularly. Attempts to bring this anger out into the open in our sessions failed. The family, according to her, were split down the middle about expressing their feelings and she was in the middle, she thought.

Going home for holidays was both dreaded and longed for – the worse part she felt was coming back to university and having to give up her mother and her sister. She was curious to know about sexual experiences with boys, but would recoil if a boy touched her. This rather outlandish looking young woman also liked to read Mills and Boon novels and was writing a romantic novel. She was aware that boys would notice her more if she put on weight and she wanted to avoid their attention. I got the impression that she and her siblings had lived quite an imaginative life as children – writing stories they shared and reading the same books. She treated me a bit like a twin too – how do people cope with conflict she once asked and did I have conflicts at all? One of her poems was about how she felt when she was hungry – how like a wolf she became. She also told me how she had been born with a damaged mouth and believed that her sister had injured it in the womb.

After a few months, Peta had begun to wash her hair and had put on a few pounds and was looking the better for it. She was thrilled too that her friend had wanted to share a house with her the next academic year. She went home for a very long summer break. When she returned she was furious. She had put on six pounds more so she now weighed five stone and eight pounds, and felt horrified. She wanted an explanation of why she had 'ballooned out' and felt the GP and I had betrayed her by letting her get this fat. We had a very tense and difficult session and she left having arranged to see me for the rest of the year. That was the last I saw of her and she did not respond to a letter I sent a few weeks later.

A year or two after this session I was consulted by a young woman who had just gone back to her studies after taking a year out. She told me that I had been seeing her housemate (evidently Peta) who was anorexic and whom she had been supporting. Peta had now graduated but this young woman had collapsed under the strain and had taken time off from her studies! She wanted help to get back on course.

Looking back it seems clear that Peta had a voracious hunger for her object; in fact, she was hungry like a wolf. The belief she held that her sister had damaged her mouth in the womb may suggest that a powerful phantasy was at work about retribution for her oral sadism. Again, the psychotherapy of this young woman was not completed.

## Susan: short-term therapy

Some anorexics do very well if they can find someone to talk to at a time when they feel ready to give up their self-starving. Susan had only been anorexic for a year and though slim had never been at a dangerously low weight, although she had stopped menstruating. She was the only child of African-Caribbean parents who had never been happy together and who had divorced three years ago when she was doing her 'A' levels. She had thrown herself into academic work and this had helped her get through a difficult transition. Susan had lived with her mother, a school secretary who ran a tight ship at home and at work. Mother had remarried a man who seemed to detest Susan though I only have her word for it. Mother had insisted that all links to father were severed after the divorce so if Susan wanted to be in contact she had to travel to his new home in London. Father had met a younger woman and started another family, in which he seemed to be happy. Susan would stay with him but found managing her feelings of jealousy about her stepsister devastating. She witnessed father being playful and relaxed with his young daughter in a way she had never imagined could be possible. Susan had left home to train as a teacher but returned regularly and was very involved with her mother who wanted her to do well. At college, Susan spent all the time working but had discovered that she could not keep up with her assignments. By this I do really mean all the time: 12 hours a day. She had been living mainly on apples, but had got to know a boy who shared the house. He had started to get her to eat an occasional half teacake and to take breaks from work. She realised she had to give up her eating problem and her obsessional approach to work or she would lose his friendship.

I saw Susan once a week for a year. She was less disturbed than many anorexics – more like the anorexics Sours saw as suffering a transient form of eating disorder. Her difficulties seemed to have developed relatively late in her life – both the anorexia and the family's turbulence. She had a relationship with both parents though mother was sometimes thoughtless about her daughter's needs. The main concerns were the stepfather's hostility and mother's expectations that Susan would put up with it. Susan's boyfriend came from a large, high-achieving family who intimidated her but who seemed to have accepted her as a prospective member of their family. Mainly listening and occasionally responding when appropriate, with an analytic interpretation seemed to benefit Susan. Some readers might feel that the changes she made in her life (she worked a bit less, went out more, put on a little weight, got engaged, began a sexual relationship with her boyfriend) were a result of the positive transference. Or it might be thought that Susan was not very disturbed and would have got better anyway. I am not so sure of either. It seems important that with anorexics, especially young people, the therapist has to have a light touch and work at the best level to make sense of the material. Lawrence (1984) described how lonely anorexics can feel and how simply listening analytically and responding can help. Bruch certainly supported a less analytic approach. However, it depends on what the patient is presenting. Perhaps what Bruch objected to is what any good therapist would object to – force-feeding interpretations that are wrong, or badly timed or addressed to the wrong level or part of the patient's personality.

Some key points

- There are different anorexic groups, varying in levels of pathology.
- Pre-oedipal, oedipal, and issues to do with later transitions, may all be present.
- Liaison with GPs is necessary if someone is at risk. Keeping out of a re-feeding regimen may be best, though Bruch disagrees.
- It may not be possible to complete therapy to the therapist's satisfaction.
- Tact is one of the most important qualities of a therapist when dealing with an anorexic – avoid forcing ideas on the anorexic or telling her what to do.
- Acceptance of the patient's ambivalence is essential and should be made explicit.
- Anorexics fear intrusion but project intrusively into the therapist.
- Starting therapy requires constructing a holding environment.
- Listening and translating anorexic symptoms into ordinary everyday concerns helps the anorexic give up her illness.
- Anorexics' loneliness and lack of self-confidence should not be underestimated neither should their destructiveness.

# 4

# BULIMIA NERVOSA

Bulimia Nervosa was not fully distinguished from anorexia as a clinical condition, until Gerald Russell published a paper on it in the UK in 1979, though it has been associated with anorexia since the early writings of Gull (1873). Bulimia nervosa has been described as 'a syndrome characterised by repeated bouts of overeating and an excessive preoccupation with the control of body weight, leading to a pattern of overeating followed by vomiting or use of purgatives ... often but not always with a history of an earlier episode of anorexia nervosa' (ICD-10, p. 352). For a diagnosis to be made, the following should all be present:

- Persistent preoccupation with eating and an irresistible craving for food with bouts of overeating in which large amounts of food are consumed in a short period of time.
- Behaviour designed to counteract the effects of the above by using one or more of the following: self-induced vomiting, purging, alternating periods of starvation, use of appetite suppressants, thyroid preparations or diuretics.
- A morbid fear of fatness with a low target weight set.

Another variant, atypical bulimia nervosa, has been distinguished as similar but 'without a significant weight change or the typical over concern about body shape and weight may be absent' (ICD-10, p. 353). The Royal College of Psychiatrists (2000) commissioned a survey of services for people with eating disorders and found 'many cases represent intermediate forms' (2000: 11) and would not fit neatly into their categories of anorexia nervosa, bulimia nervosa and binge eating disorder. This latter is 'bingeing without compensatory behaviour', and is associated with obesity and increased mortality rate.

People who binge and vomit or who purge may also have enlarged salivary glands, electrolyte imbalance which can predispose them to fits and cramps, and they may have damaged the enamel on their teeth by vomiting. They may also develop long-term constipation, though short-term they are likely to have stomach cramps and diarrhoea. If they restrict their food intake too, they may have the additional symptoms outlined in Chapter 3.

In Chapter 3 some thought was given to whether or not anorexia should be considered as distinct from bulimia. Much of the clinical literature on anorexia and bulimia does not differentiate. However, I do want to tease out some differences, for the sake of clarity, even though this may be vexing. The Royal College of Psychiatrists' Report clarified how they discriminated between different groups of patients with eating disorder when they were looking at service provision in the UK. They described anorexia nervosa as characterised by low weight, morbid fear of fat and amenorrhoea (cessation of periods). It was associated with high mortality, morbidity, chronicity and commonly, with depression. Bulimia was characterised by normal or increased weight, binges, vomiting (or other compensatory behaviours) and body image psychopathology. They linked bulimia to hidden physical complications and depression. The mortality rate was deemed to be unknown. Clearly, one reason to distinguish these different configurations of symptoms was to make sure that those at most risk got the appropriate help they needed as soon as possible. Indeed, the report tells us that 'Eating disorders are associated with high mortality. The Standardised Mortality Rate (SMR) for eating disorders ... has been estimated at 538, compared with 136–197 for depression, schizophrenia and alcoholism' (Harris and Barraclough, 1998, cited in Royal College of Psychiatry, 2000: 11).

Farrell (1995) considered the different categories where anorexia and bulimia are concerned and noted the confusions created by traditional classifications since anorexics may vomit and bulimics may be thin and restrict their food intake. She rejected the term 'bulimarexia' used by Boskind-White and White (1987) and declined to refer to 'bingers and purgers' or to use the term 'bulimia nervosa' which was first used by Russell (1979) because she said the usage of both terms is inconsistent in the literature. She opted instead for three categories: 'anorexics', meaning diet restricting anorexics; anorexic bulimics or bulimic anorexics; and a third category, 'bulimics' to refer to 'normal' weight bulimics. For the purposes of this chapter, I will use the term, bulimic, to represent Farrell's last two groups, that is, people who take in food but then use laxatives or vomiting to expel it, whatever their weight. If I want to draw attention to 'normal' weight bulimics I will specify them as such, with the apostrophes indicating the problematic nature of 'normal' weight. The difficulty in drawing clear boundaries around these different categories encourages caution – the links suggested by Sohn may be more helpful in practice.

## The psychodynamics of bulimia

Schwartz identified several subtly differentiated understandings of bulimia in the psychoanalytic literature. The first, represented by writers such as Rizzuto, emphasised the need to eat as a dissociated search for the breast and the need to vomit as the impulse to get rid of the self who has the need (personal communication cited in Schwartz, 1986). The second linked this same difficulty to an ensuing problem in separating and individuating from the mother (Sugarman and Kurash, 1981). A third, outlined by Schwartz, extended the idea that bulimia reflected an arrest at an early stage of development of transitional object formation, with a resulting fixation on one's own body in lieu of an external object. There were consequences thus for symbolisation, boundary formation and individuation. Farrell (1995) developed this idea further, and argued that taking in too much food is a way of connecting with mother, creating a special kind of transitional time. Vomit and rituals about clearing up may serve as transitional phenomena. Schwartz stressed the role of defective individuation in the failure to gain a historical perspective on one's own body. This affected a sense of potential space and symbolisation – the bulimic feels her body is her mother's. Sugarman put it this way: 'Gorging became identified as an act of symbiotic reunion, vomiting as an act of separation from, if not annihilation of mother' (Sugarman and Kurash, 1981: 65).

Furthermore, the role of the mother, in all the American eating disorder literature from the earlier period, emphasised that there really was a domineering, pathogenic mother. This literature comes from a clinical context when the eating disorders were seen as psychosomatic disorders and were linked to a mother who could not allow separation. Sours agreed with the depiction of a problematic relationship with a real omnipotent mother but drew attention to the role of fathers (Sours, 1980: 319–20). A fuller discussion of psychosomatic disorders and their relation to eating disorders is found in Chapter 7.

The conceptualisations just mentioned are based on a developmental or interpersonal deficit model of pathology. Conflictual models stress how the individual deals with unacceptable wishes and fears, represses or splits them off or finds ways of making compromises which satisfy some unconscious wishes while appeasing that part of the mind that finds them unacceptable. Much of the literature was about oral fixation in both anorexia and bulimia. In Freud's letters to Fliess, he identified a fantasy of pregnancy, conceived orally, but which had to be destroyed, as a self-punishment, by vomiting (Freud, 1899). A baby can be acquired, in this infantile fantasy, via kissing or eating – Freud later linked it to the oral forerunner of the Oedipus complex. There is a wish to get a baby, displaced upwards to the mouth as the receptive organ, followed by expulsion of the imagined paternal phallus, in a turn away from this wish and a rejection of the ingested phallus/baby/food.

Ideas such as these were built on by various psychoanalysts since Freud, including Kestenberg (1968) and Sperling (1983). This last writer saw the wish to castrate the father by oral incorporation of the phallus as the principal motive and stresses the oral sadistic aspect of the symptom rather than the receptive aspect, linking it to a wish to control mother by possessing father's penis. However, it may also be the daughter's frustrated wish for father that has led to a regression to an oral mode of relating to him (Sachs, 1929). The fixation at the oral stage impedes the development of the superego which remains 'biting', as has been noted in bulimics who can be so self-critical, and interferes with the process of sublimation and renunciation of sexual wishes towards the father, leaving them prone to impulsive acting out.

Krueger (1988) saw bulimia as consumption of a good object/ mother and the expulsion of a bad one as part of a magical quest to restore a good self-object bond and to overcome destructiveness. This is doomed to failure because of an incapacity to satisfactorily mourn the damaged object. Sprince (1988) identified the fear of engulfment and abandonment as factors that interfere with a fantasy of a merger with mother which would put everything right in the bulimic's mind.

Schwartz suggested that eating-disordered people have been exposed to 'primal-scene stimuli' (1986: 447) which they may then react against by doing to oneself (as in sticking a finger down the throat to induce vomiting) what was perceived once as happening genitally between the parents. This would involve several reversals: Oedipal exclusion would be overcome; passive wishes would be turned into active ones; recognition of the lack of a penis would be avoided in the girl or castration would be denied in the boy. If what

Schwartz argued is correct, the bulimic has found a way of not only denying castration or lack of a penis but he or she also escapes the existential and psychic imperative of identifying as either male or female – he or she is both in unconscious phantasy in the binge–purge enactment.

Bingeing and vomiting can be seen as a kind of unconscious masturbatory activity. They often involve an excitement that makes the unconscious sexual dimension evident. Schwartz listed a series of objects, identified as equivalents to food in their capacity to be related to in a similar frantic way, including horses, dolls, art work and (I would add), reading and academic work. Stealing may serve a similar function too and often clothes and food are the goods chosen. External objects may also organise and help pull together the individual's internal world as described by Hamburg (1989). This use of an external object keeps the bulimic tied to dependence on an outside object rather than enabling him or her to work through their oedipal strivings in a way that will allow him or her to secure satisfactions with a partner of their own in a more adult form of sexuality. Lefebvre concurs with Schwartz's view of bulimia as oral hunger masking genital arousal and adds that in his own practice he has found 'alimentary anorexia is often a defence against genital bulimia' (Lefebvre, 1991: 475).

Regurgitation of food often involves rituals around the toilet and bathroom. This and the use of laxatives by some bulimics has been considered in relation to anal conflicts and, again viewed as a regression away from genitality and linked to unmanageable defiance and hostility. Oliner (1982) supported the view that bulimia is an anal-sadistic attack on the self instead of an object that is felt to be faecal.

## Contemporary perspectives

Reich and Cierpka reviewed the psychodynamic literature on bulimia from a more contemporary, European point of view, starting from the premise that bulimia is 'an elaborated habitualised impulsive action' (Habermas, 1990), a form of impulsive neurosis as described by Fenichel (1945). This action permits internal tension to be dealt with by means of physical objects and according to the authors 'lies between an involuntary symptom, an unconscious intrapsychic defence and a sanctioned cultural technique' (Reich and Cierpka, 1998: 383). They suggested it is sometimes felt as ego-syntonic and at other times as ego-dystonic (that is, it feels OK one moment and is unacceptable to the sufferer at other moments). The reason for the switch is a deep-seated identity conflict between two contradictory parts of the self. The first part is the ideal – that which is often most apparent to acquaintances of bulimic people: they are active, independent, in control of themselves. The second part is weak, needy, lacking in control and felt as a shameful secret defective self. The sense of an inner fault is core. The authors found disturbances in bulimics originate not only in the pre-oedipal period but throughout childhood and adolescence with basic needs for approval, attachment, intimacy and affective resonance, unmet or even derided. Bulimic symptoms may be extensive and part of a larger serious clinical picture in personality disorder (see Reich, 1997) or can be found in people who are otherwise undisturbed. Assumptions should not be made in advance about the overall clinical picture.

Reich and Cierpka discussed the role of sexual abuse in the aetiology of bulimia and find that it is no more frequent than in other severe mental illnesses but is nonetheless considerable. What they found more potent was a 'central fear ... that every form of intimacy culminates in betrayal' (1998: 386) and that bulimics find themselves in persisting Oedipal conflict situations, often against a background of extreme marital tension. There is some evidence of increased incidence of physical abuse in the families of bulimics (Schmidt, Humfress and Treasure, 1997).

The Oedipal constellations Reich and Cierpka described include:

- an idealised father and a mother seen as an adversary
- a despised father and a mother seen as an adversary
- a distant, unreliable father and a helpless mother

Traumatisation and overstimulation can ensue from an eroticised relationship with the father. There are contradictory superego demands that are hard to cope with – a wish for approval and to conform, and yet impulsive behaviour and rebelliousness. Defences used by bulimics include reversal into opposites; in particular, feelings and passivity into activity, in order to avoid experiencing conflict or difficult feelings. Identification with the aggressor is a common defence, as is denial. One especially difficult experience for the bulimic is shame, which is extensive and linked to a belief in essential defectiveness that is displaced on to the body. An ideal image of the body is held in mind and sought after as a defence against anxiety. The functions of eating are multiple – eating appears to give the individual some control though it goes against the demand of the strict superego for the perfection of the body. Mood is regulated by food but there is then counter-regulation through vomiting or purging, which erases the binge, restores the desired body image and evacuates out feelings and wishes that are unacceptable (Reich and Cierpka, 1998).

Williams (1997), developed the idea of the 'no-entry syndrome' mentioned in Chapter 3 when working with anorexics, and the idea of 'psychically porous' individuals when working with bulimics. The latter is our concern in this chapter. By porous, Williams means that such individuals have been heavily projected into by parental figures who may have been traumatised themselves and are either frightened or frightening or both. She saw similarities with the children who show disorganised, disoriented patterns of attachment, described by Main and Solomon (1986). Such parental figures cannot adequately contain their own anxieties and cannot therefore help their children with theirs.

Furthermore, such parents may project anxiety into the child. Bion (1962) believed that a mother's ability to receive and contain an infant's projections was a fundamental building block of mental health. If the mother can contain whatever disturbs and discomforts the infant, and make some sense of it emotionally, then she can feed it back to the child in a way that helps. The child can take back into itself the projected feeling, which would then have a meaning and could be managed. If we imagine the small child waking up in the dark from a dream and crying out for a mother who comes and soothes it, telling the child it will be alright, that he has just had a bad dream, we get a simplified picture of the kind of process involved. Containment of raw emotional states happens all the time in mothers of small babies, but when a mother cannot bear to have feelings projected into her, the baby gets back, not modified feelings, but something much worse and intensified: a nameless dread. The baby not only has to do without understanding but may also have an unmanageable experience pushed back into him or her. In contrast, Bion thought that when a baby introjects contained feelings he or she also introjects containment itself, which acts as an organising function within the infantile mind. This linking and thinking function brings order into the chaotic infantile psyche. Williams supposed that a parent overflowing with her own projections would bring a disorganising function into the infantile mind, again with reference to the work of Main and Solomon (1986).

Adolescence is a time when the individual is faced with an increased desire for close relationship to an object. One solution to an overwhelming desire is to hang on tighter to the original object (Anderson, 2001). Conflicts in adolescence are many and complex and are made more dangerous by the developing capacity to be sexually potent, to be physically strong and aggressive, to out-do parents, intellectually. Conflicts can involve integrative forces, bringing about order, wholeness and co-operation but they may also involve processes that deal with conflict by getting rid of difficult experiences or disavowing them. Anderson (2001) emphasised that in some severely disturbed eating-disordered patients, whether bulimic or anorexic, there are parts of the mind that function in an actively disorganising way while other parts may seek to integrate and develop. These can be thought of as psychotic and non-psychotic parts of the mind (Bion, 1957). The severe forms of eating disorder show us how the patient's mind can get gripped by psychotic functioning. Phantasies can be experienced in a concrete way and are not in contact with the more normal part of the mind that can symbolise them. The kind of difficulties adolescents develop, such as eating disorders, drug taking, self-harm, may be how such phantasies get acted out instead. Food may have an erotic meaning, for example, so cannot be tolerated because of an unconscious fear that eating involves a sexual state of mind, which is to be avoided. Anderson describes how the adolescent mind can be 'captured' by contempt for the needy self. This happens only fleetingly in normal adolescence but it can get addictive and the whole personality gets captured, leaving the therapist to hold onto and contain the normal part of the personality.

## Borderline personality disorder

Some clinicians have commented on adult patients with eating disorders who also exhibit qualities, symptoms or behaviour associated with borderline personality disorder. Bulimics are more likely than anorexics to fit the description of borderline personality disorder. An estimated 30 per cent of bulimics fulfil the criteria set out in a range of studies when these are subjected to the Diagnostic Interview for Borderline Patients (DIB) (see Dennis and Sansone, 1991). There is much controversy around the classification of personality disorders but the pertinent issue here is the extent to which some of our bulimic patients might suffer from the following problems taken from Diagnostic and Statistical Manual of Mental Disorder (DSM IV):

- unstable and intense personal relationships
- potentially self-damaging impulsivity

- emotional instability
- inappropriate, intense anger
- recurrent suicidal threats or gestures
- marked and persistent identity disturbances
- chronic feelings of emptiness or boredom
- fears of abandonment (APA, 1994)

Strictly speaking, a patient would need to fit at least five of these criteria to be considered as having a borderline personality disorder. For me the list is striking in that many people with a serious eating disorder would fulfil five of these criteria, at some stage in their lives. Johnson (1991) suggested that he, too, has found these features in many patients and that the main difference between the subgroup of bulimics who fit this description and those who do not, is that outcome may be less positive after treatment for the former. Another difference is that laxative abuse was practised more by people who had borderline personality, perhaps 'because the function is more in the service of self-integration or self-punishment than simple weight regulation' (Johnson, 1991: 174). When it comes to technique, some clinicians recommend particular approaches for people who might have borderline personality disorder. I discuss technical modifications further in Chapter 6.

Sohn (1985) not only challenged the distinction between bulimia and anorexia, given the appearance in the clinical situation of both anorexic and bulimic states of mind but also drew a comparison between them and borderline personality disordered patients. He described all these patients as having a superficial interest in what the analyst has to offer them and a preference for their own way of understanding, so much so that it infects clinicians who become 'bland' and 'smug' about their work (1986: 56). Psychoanalytic therapy confronts such patients with opportunities to experience something very new but, he writes glumly: 'The specificity of their psychoanalyst is the red rag to the bull of their envious denials and strivings so that the analytic seriousness of purpose and interest is attacked and nullified' (1985: 56).

Hamburg discussed the complex nature of deconstructing the meanings behind any individual's bulimia.

The quest for a solitary meaning is only one approach to the problem. It assumes that the mystery has one solution, one basic, hidden truth, and narrows the science of interpretation to an unveiling of this basic truth ... Unfortunately, the search for an ultimate meaning denies the complexity of the psychiatric symptom. In confronting the inevitable competition of different contexts and interpretations we need to ask whether the function of a symptom might not be precisely to weave together diverse contexts into a single metaphoric fabric. By deferring the search for one correct interpretation and instead examining the relationship among several meanings of a symptom we might learn more about the symptom's capacity to integrate aspects of the patient's world. (Hamburg, 1989: 132)

In his view that the symptom reveals the trace of a falling apart and a recovery from the fall, he is echoing Freud's early ideas about a psychosis (Freud, 1911). This puts bulimia in a closer relationship to psychosis as other commentators have done when discussing it in relation to borderline disorders. Hamburg wrote: 'There is a loss of space in this falling-together, a collapse of a richer world into a smaller, poorer one. The body becomes a fortress to contain further collapse ... there is a developmental retreat that blends spaces, zones, and desires into a less differentiated amalgam' (Hamburg, 1989: 134–5). Thus bulimia collapses experience into orality, anality and genitality. I will illustrate some of these points by way of clinical examples.

## Michael: a boy who never stopped running (a failed brief engagement with a group)

Michael was referred to a group I ran with a colleague in a day hospital. He had been bulimic since he was 15 and was now aged 27. He had moved to the city from another part of the country, to live with relatives. He was estranged from his mother, a single parent who had a drink problem. He had lived with a variety of stepfather figures in his family and had ended up on bad terms with them all, some of whom were violent and abusive. He liked cooking and would cook for the whole family, but secretly would take food and chew it and then put it back in the pot so when the family sat down to dinner again they would sometimes unknowingly get what he had already had in his mouth. Although quite amenable and forthcoming when spoken to on an individual basis, he was reluctant to join a group. Michael preferred to talk to someone individually and to make pottery. He was an inpatient as was another member of the group and the others were outpatients. My colleague assessed Michael, at the invitation of his psychiatrist and thought that he would be challenging in the group but that it would be advantageous to include another man as the only male participant seemed isolated. Michael had become rather a special figure on the ward and his care had been championed by a group of nurses who were committed to creating a better, more patient-centred milieu. His talent at making art also singled him out. He was articulate and likeable, too. He exercised frantically and was very thin. The regime on the ward was different for different patients, depending on the consultant psychiatrist under whose care the patient came and the nurse who was the keyworker. It was felt that he should be allowed to eat and drink whenever and whatever he wanted and to vomit, but the staff would talk to him about why he was doing it. Another group of nurses felt his capacity to manipulate should be challenged. They wanted to insist he attend therapeutic groups and to tackle more forcefully how he avoided food or secretly vomited.

When Michael first joined the group, he decided he was against sitting on a chair and sat on the floor. Another patient opted to do the same so that after a while everyone was on the floor except for the two people running the group. We tried to get the group to think about what this meant and after a while, Michael opted to sit on a chair and most of the others followed suit. The other male member of the group was not present at this or the subsequent meeting. At the next meeting of the group, Michael sat in a chair opposite me. The group talked about how angry they had become at various times with their siblings and some people volunteered information about their rage towards members of their family. The group was talkative and individuals seemed to bond together in the light of shared experience of violent and murderous feelings. However, Michael could not stand it and leapt to his feet with his fist clenched and ran at me from across the room as if to punch me. He ran past me and punched the wall behind me, making a large dent, before leaving the group and going back to the ward. The group members were very frightened – talk had collapsed into action and the safe space of the group had become like a family space where fighting was for real. Despite our invitation to come back to the group, Michael never did.

Readers will have all sorts of ideas about what this episode meant for Michael and what was going on in the group but I mention it here to draw attention to the levels of impulsivity in some bulimic patients which can be difficult to manage. Michael could not contain his emotions, and we were not able to contain him in the group. Furthermore, he was not contained on the ward. I think he experienced me in the group as a bad parent attacking him by my presence (I had not spoken much at all), in a very concrete way. I saw Michael running around the city streets for several years after this occasion, still very thin and looking hunted. After having been made a special patient who then failed to progress, he became identified with mental health advocacy, but did not seem to benefit from that either. He is, perhaps an example of a patient in whom bulimia is linked to a borderline personality with many of the features described in the DSM IV. I think we may have held him better in a group with another man present or if he had been more contained on the ward. An individual therapy may have helped him better still. The capacity of eating-disordered patients to split off and project their feelings can make for a very divided ward when they are in-patients, unless the staff can find a way of understanding and working with the projections.

## Ellen: a four-year, once-a-week therapy

I first met Ellen when she appeared in a student counselling service as an emergency referral. She was going to leave university for a term because she had become ill with suspected lupus erythmatosis and had fallen behind with her work. She wanted to talk to someone because she was so worried about her health and how it might affect her return to study. She was a local young woman, in her late twenties, with a shock of curly red hair, of medium build and with a very serious demeanour. She was quite agitated as she spoke about feeling so forlorn because she had managed to get into a prestigious nursing school when she was 17 and had found the work and the atmosphere too stressful and had dropped out. She was afraid illness, whatever it turned out to be, would hold her back at this second attempt to get a qualification and a good career. She had felt ill for over a year and had wondered if she was depressed. She felt she had no control over herself, was arguing all the time with her boyfriend and felt tired and unable to concentrate on anything. She thought if she could talk to me that it would take the strain off her boyfriend who had been very supportive but who was stressed by his studies. She thought she should mention that when she was much younger she had been bulimic and had been quite unhappy in her family. Everything was better now and she had a much better self-image, though she was convinced the steroids she was taking for lupus were making her face look puffy. I offered to see Ellen again.

When Ellen returned the next week she told me about a series of illnesses she had suffered when younger. I began to wonder whether she was simply physically ill or whether there was a psychosomatic dimension or, it flitted through my mind, that she might be someone who converts her psychic distress into physical expressions in a more hysteric-like way. Her appointment for more tests to confirm the diagnosis of her illness had been postponed another week and she was angry about this. She said she wasn't in the mood for talking this week, though it had helped a lot last week and her relationship to her boyfriend had felt less under pressure. She went on to describe at length her physical symptoms and I started to feel as if she wanted to get rid of them by dumping them on me. I ventured an interpretation about the bad feelings created by her illness making her want to be able to vomit them out like she would have done when she vomited food out when she was bulimic. She seemed to find this containing and asked to come again while she was waiting for the results.

The next week was the last week before a break and she had received confirmation that she would have to go into hospital for tests. She talked about her family never taking her seriously and how her aunt says what is wrong with her is stress but does so in a way that doesn't help and makes her feel put down. She was curious after the last meeting about what had happened to her bulimia. She wondered if she could come back after her leave of absence and see me regularly. Meanwhile she needed to get better physically and survive the next period. I agreed, and during the leave she wrote telling me she definitely had lupus and not cancer, which she had convinced herself could be possible, and felt she would like psychotherapy, if I could offer it to her.

Ellen's therapy started a few months later and was always once-a-week. The first three counselling sessions had helped me to assess her suitability for a more psychoanalytically orientated psychotherapy. Ellen returned from leave of absence with a wish to understand more about her bulimia which she said had stopped when she thought she might have cancer but had started up again. She was vomiting several times a week. She was also anxious about being able to complete satisfactorily her repeat first year at university and wanted help with the relationship with her boyfriend, which could get quite violent, emotionally. The fierceness of Ellen's emotional reactions became a hallmark of her therapy.

Right from the first session of counselling there was a marked tendency for the sessions to alternate in flavour whereby I felt something I did helped was followed in the next meeting, with a sense that often, whatever I did made matters worse. This was not completely predictable: sometimes we had a run of sessions when I was found to be helpful or hateful but there was always, eventually, a tendency to swing between two opposite feelings. By the end of the therapy this had become mitigated but was still in existence. I came to regard this process as linked to what Woodmansey (1966) called an 'alternating transference' and I recognised it as related to the ambivalence associated with bulimia. What I said was taken in, found to be satisfying and then later something would turn the satisfaction into rejection and whatever I said was spat back at me, or secretly gotten rid of by some private method. Ellen often went to the toilet before she left the building where she saw me and I wondered if she was literally vomiting up what she had taken in or perhaps, urinating on it and flushing it down the loo. It was a long time before I noticed this tendency. I considered commenting on it but thought twice – what she did after the session and didn't tell me about seemed private and I didn't want to intrude. However, not commenting on it could be seen as collusive. What I did do was to pick up on how she got rid of the value of what I said, or sometimes what she thought, whenever it happened in the sessions, when it seemed appropriate. The pattern to Ellen's therapy is very common when working with people who are bulimic but it was more intense in Ellen, partly, I think because she was taking steroids, which can make people feel almost homicidal when they are angry.

Some background to Ellen may help us appreciate better what her therapy involved. Ellen was the middle child of professional parents. She had a brother who was two years older and a sister two years younger. Ellen had been the odd one out in her family who were all dedicated sports people. She had never liked team games or sport and was drawn more to art and poetry. She was lonely at school, had been fat and was bullied. She had been seen by her parents as overdramatising normal everyday events and making too much fuss. Her parents encouraged her to make friends with her bullies and went to great efforts to invite them round for tea and to ensure their daughter was not intimidated by them. However, this didn't work and left Ellen feeling more isolated and betrayed. She was compliant but developed anorexia nervosa at the age of 11 and was seen briefly by her family doctor. She started eating again, but sometimes made herself vomit. When she changed schools she adopted a more defiant, rebellious stance, experimenting with sex and drugs. She put herself at risk with a variety of sexual partners and only just managed to get enough work done to get into nurse-training, mainly as a way of leaving home. As the therapy progressed it became apparent that Ellen's difficulties at home had started much earlier.

Ellen's mother had always felt strongly about self-control and discipline. She had been an amateur athlete who was proud of her boyish shape and had not enjoyed having babies. She had, nonetheless, applied herself to bringing up her children much as she had her sports training – the children were regimented and organised with strict routines. Her husband wanted the family to give an excellent impression to the outside world – a bit like a top athletics team. The family were well known in their area and people looked up to the parents. Behind the scenes, the family were quite different. From an early age, Ellen had felt as if no one ever listened to her when she talked. She remembered showing her mother a picture she had made at school and mother glancing at it briefly then throwing it in the bin. This memory summed up Ellen's feelings about how she had been seen at home – a rather useless and messy thing.

Frequently, Ellen had been left behind as the family went off on sporting engagements and events. Ellen had been left with a number of people who looked after her. One was an older cousin of her mother's who was old-fashioned and strict. This woman was feared by Ellen. Another woman, an old school friend of her mother's, was also called on regularly to take care of her. This woman liked music and took Ellen to concerts and became a trusted and reliable support. However, she moved away to take care of her elderly parents when Ellen was ten years old. There was also a beloved grandfather who lived at some distance away from Ellen's family. Summers at his house had been happy experiences.

Ellen had a complicated relationship with her father. She knew she didn't get on with her mother but her father was sometimes a good figure in her mind – one she felt more understood by but one who made her very confused about her feelings. As the therapy progressed, Ellen told of times as she was growing up when she felt she and her father had a special relationship – they shared a love of music and this sometimes set them apart from the rest of the family. As she got older, she described scenes, which expressed her doubts about their relationship. Ellen's father didn't like the children to lock the bathroom door – he wanted to be able to get in any room he wanted at any time. Even when she was 13 years old, he would come in the bathroom as she was bathing and look at her naked body while chatting, as if it were all very normal. She would feel ashamed of her developing body and feel stupid for being embarrassed. As she got older their relationship seemed to grow more distant though on occasions he offered her opportunities to go away to concerts with him which she didn't take up on her own. As a teenager, she got into fierce arguments with both parents and felt they were both pleased when she left home at 17 and had much less contact with them.

Once Ellen had dropped out of nursing school she became involved in the drug scene in a big way and had shared a house with someone who used heroin. She got involved with him and started smoking heroin herself, though she did not become an addict. She also took an overdose when he became involved with someone else and she had to move out. While she was recovering from this and having seen a psychiatrist for a few sessions she met her current boyfriend who knew the people she had lived with and who also occasionally smoked heroin and who offered her somewhere to stay. He was some ten years older than her, and they developed a relationship, which sounded at first like a parent–child relationship, but as therapy progressed I discovered that sometimes they were physically violent to each other. Despite the inauspicious beginnings, this relationship developed and they stayed together although he sometimes hit her when she provoked him (her words not mine). They got involved in making and selling clothes for the club scene. They both realised as time went on that they wanted to go to university and took an access course which led to them both starting as mature students at the same time, though in different universities.

As therapy progressed several themes emerged and would have to be worked through again and again. The first and most dominant aspect was the sense Ellen had that she could be rejected at any time or could reject me at any time. The second was that she felt she couldn't understand her memories especially some shadowy ones, which seemed sexual and she didn't know what to make of them. In addition, she still experienced some odd sensations she could not understand. Both of these themes were also linked to an issue about truth and reality – could I be of any use if how I understood her was independent of her version of the truth? Could I be trusted if I had a mind of my own? Could truth be more complex than the black and white versions she tussled over with her parents? In order to emphasise what seems most pertinent and can be generalised about in relation to other patients I will focus on these in this chapter.

### You don't want me – I don't want you

Almost from day one, after a session in which I felt I had made an emotional contact either immediately or in the next meeting, I would discover Ellen thought that therapy was a waste of time or that I had said something critical to her and was trying to get rid of her. After Ellen told me about the extent of violence that had occurred between her and her boyfriend, Rory, she was convinced I would either not believe her or believe her and think she was too sordid to carry on seeing. When I tried to understand what she said to me and feed it back to her in an interpretation or even in a more clarifying way, she thought it was an attack on her or on her parents. She thought she must be essentially bad because they had brought her up in the same way that they had brought up their other two children and it had worked for them – both siblings were happy and well adjusted. She believed that if I gave her any help there would be punishment to follow. Indeed, this was true since when I was helpful she would react aggressively against me or attack herself. This sadomasochistic style of relating to me and to herself was deeply engrained. Once when she had been attacking herself with incriminations about her badness which I had interpreted she went silent for a long time and then said she felt stuck. She was tired and wanted to curl up like a baby, and did not want to listen to what I said. I linked this to how it was like trying to feed an upset baby who struggled and wanted to avoid taking anything in and so felt even hungrier and undernourished, yet if anything good got through she felt it must be poisonous. However, this kind of interpretation was like a goad to Ellen. She said she could never imagine anyone else feeding her and that when I raised ideas like that it was to taunt her with something that would be impossible for her – I was being sadistic. She then went on talk about some further medical explorations which had to be undertaken in hospital, as if there was a link between treatment and a kind of sadistic pleasure for the professional involved.

The same process of having a good experience, which then turns bad, was detectable in most aspects of Ellen's life but even so, the general trend, during the therapy, was for the bad to get less bad and the good to get better. An example was Ellen's academic work. She was genuinely very interested in her subject, sociology. She worked hard and enthusiastically and was successful. Nonetheless, every exam or assessed piece of work made her feel convinced she had failed. Sometimes I felt as if I had to gear myself up for a crisis, expecting her to have failed an end-of-year exam because of the severity of her self-criticisms only to find she had got top marks. Ellen's fears were deeply felt and she would get gripped by a fatal pessimism which had an impact in the countertransference. Her fears were real but the causes were not in the real world but in unconscious phantasy. The extreme discrepancy between what was objectively happening to her and the shadow it cast on her unconscious functioning, affected the therapy greatly. She objected to almost everything I said although not always immediately. As we went on, Ellen became able to shift her position so that we could collaborate on creating some understanding together. The analogy that comes to mind is from my amateur attempts to teach myself guitar – when you tune the guitar, using an electronic tuner, the arrow on the dial shoots right past the desired mid-point and when you try to compensate it shoots past in the opposite way. Eventually you get it right but it doesn't stay that way long and when you tune the next string, its always worth checking whether the other ones still sound right.

Ellen sometimes talked about how her parents' visits were always stressful, but she began to be able to develop strategies with her boyfriend for how they were going to deal with the parents' perceived intrusiveness. I was impressed with the way the two could co-operate despite ongoing turbulence between the two of them. The violence between them became less physical though still, at times, very hurtful. However, there continued, for the first year at least, to be a dilemma. When she talked about her parents and their behaviour, I tried to pick up what was meaningful from it in the transference. This would help and then she would explode and say I didn't believe her about how they had treated her and I was saying it was all her fault. If I said something more empathic to her about her experiences she would later explode because she thought her parents were alright and it was she who was in the wrong and these were only 'stories' she was telling me. The stories she did tell me were about parents who interfered and were hurtful to her and to her boyfriend – he found them extraordinarily meddlesome, according to Ellen.

## Sexual phantasms

As time went on, Ellen's conviction that I wanted to get rid of her altered: sometimes I also wanted to laugh at her, she thought. She struggled over what to think about what she said to me and what I said to her. Fragments of memory or fantasy – we never did finalise what they were – reappeared at various times. She had a memory of being given enemas by her mother's cousin and assumed all children had these. Her bottom would get sore too when she was a child but she didn't know why. She had a vague memory but didn't know if it was real, of something being put in her vagina by someone. I tried to understand what was being communicated: when these phenomena appeared and why they did. I explored what they told us was happening between us at any time, without denying they could be memories of abuse. At the time there was a lot of discussion in the press and on Ellen's course, about False Memory Syndrome. It was a delicate matter and I felt helped by a part of Ellen who was beginning to be able to think with me about grey areas. At times, she felt I wasn't simply taking everything she said at face value or doing the opposite, negating it, or using it as a reason to get rid of her or to laugh at her. I am struck by how Hamburg's ideas about the function of bulimia to weave together a broken down inner world so aptly describe what I found with Ellen. Hamburg believes that therapists need to balance respect for the architect of the symptom with compassion for the sufferer so that there is a 'falling-together rather than falling apart' (Hamburg, 1989: 137).

Ellen gradually ceased to vomit and binge. When she brought the subject into the sessions we thought about its meanings but, on the whole, it seemed less potent than our relationship for expressing the ebbs and flows of Ellen's inner world. As her vomiting came to an end Ellen felt much worse most of the time. Her academic work seemed to take on some qualities that had previously attached themselves to bingeing and vomiting. She would binge on work and then feel exhausted and so stuffed she couldn't think. She would avoid work and be unprepared for her assignments. She would vomit up all her anxieties about it to me and to her boyfriend. Over time she was able to create a calmer inner space where she could take in and think about her subject. I think she began to feel that when she was empty and hollow inside emotionally that she could bear it for a while – she was no longer quite alone, though she was often miserable. She had someone to turn to, if she could wait, and she could explore her feelings and elaborate her thoughts.

Ellen turned out to be a gifted student and I enjoyed her original cast of mind. As Ellen became more successful, her anxieties about competing with other people came to the fore, especially as she had always felt her parents preferred their son in particular, and did not take her academic efforts seriously. Her brother had done very well and was working as an academic in another country and rarely saw his family. Her sister, who had appeared to be so preferred and happy turned out to have had some serious emotional problems herself and the relationship with Ellen vastly improved. Ellen felt doing well at university was the equivalent of being like a boy and felt very cut down to size whenever her achievements failed to convince her she was as good as her brother. As a range of feelings, beyond 'I am bad, you don't want me', emerged, Ellen's 'hunger' for her therapy began to surface. She became incensed about breaks and enraged that she had to fit in with my routines and that I didn't tell her about myself. She became jealous about sharing me while all the time denying my value in any links I made in the transference. She would also attack herself for wanting more of me than she could have and believed this confirmed her fear she was as bad as she said her mother had always told her she was. She wanted to have more of me and shut me out at the same time. She would rant at me if I interpreted this and then get depressed about how she treated me.

When she had gained some stability, there ensued occasions when Ellen had an experience in the session which would be called a flash back, if it was centred on an actual experience, or a kind of acting out, if such an experience had not concretely taken place. These terms don't do justice to the experience she and I had, and perhaps, the term enactment conveys a hint of what they felt like but has its drawbacks too (see Perelberg and Levinson, 2003). Ellen had the feeling that something was being put into her on more than one occasion, in a literal way. It was sometimes down her throat and sometimes in her bottom or vagina. She reacted as if she were being violated and was very frightened. In enactments, the therapist contributes to the problem. Some people think that, in a way, the enactment is the only way certain material can get into therapy and be thought about. I think my contribution may have simply been trying to understand her and this in itself felt like a violation and felt intrusive, however cautiously I put my thoughts to her. Ellen had told me of a place she had gone to as a child – an old, broken down building in which she could gain entry by climbing up a drainpipe and squeezing in through a damaged pane in the window. Here she would hide and feel safe from everyone. I began to feel that this was akin to what Winnicott described in children whose true self had been shrouded by a false caretaker self. This core true self had to be left alone – it was 'incognito' and trying to make contact with it was a kind of trespass that was unbearable. I told Ellen she needed me to acknowledge the vulnerable, private self but not to interfere with it in any way and she seemed to feel this made her safer.

## Ending

Ellen did very well on her course and went on to do a Master's Degree afterwards which allowed us to carry on meeting for another year. When she came to the ending of her therapy which had been predicated on her being a registered student, she found ending extremely difficult and her bulimia returned briefly. She was angry that she could not continue and furious that she wanted to. If she had been a patient in private practice we would have continued, but she wasn't, and she had to face the fact that she could not continue. Although we worked towards the ending for a long time, it was still very traumatic. We had worked successfully in that she had completed her degree, gone on to establish the beginnings of a good career, she was not bingeing or vomiting, she had got married to her boyfriend and they were planning a child. She had better relationships with her family, though she was less involved with her parents, and she felt her mind was clearer than it had ever been before. She was appreciative at times of the help I had given her. However, in our last but one meeting she told me that she had often cut herself when she had been seeing me but had never told me about it and made sure the cuts were not visible. This too had stopped now, though obviously, there was something rather 'cutting' in what she was saying to me at the last minute. We met again for a follow up session three months after she had finished and she seemed to have maintained all the gains that she had made, although she was still angry about finishing. I had, with her permission, written to her GP suggesting some alternative sources of help in the NHS: in particular, an intensive analytic group. However, she had not been to see the GP and was managing well without professional help.

## Discussion

Ellen could also be considered as someone with a borderline personality disorder as well as being bulimic. She may also have been psychosomatic. Ellen reacted in very extreme ways during her therapy, not only to interpretations which can feel threatening to many recipients, but even to clarifications and empathy. Dana and Lawrence reiterated the Freudian notion that 'poison is the nourishment that makes one ill' (1987: 193) in trying to explain what it feels like to be bulimic. Ellen felt whatever she took in from me could turn poisonous. Ellen's fear of being intruded upon and her hostility were pronounced and there was always a risk of a negative therapeutic reaction with Ellen terminating her therapy prematurely. She stayed and there took place a 'push–pull' drama akin to that described by Swift (1991: 61) as Ellen pushed me away or pulled me back in.

Readers may be pondering on whether or not Ellen had been sexually abused. Much of what she said would lead one to imagine she had, but it wasn't at all clear in her mind. It seemed that what was at issue was a clouded awareness of not knowing what was being done to her and what unconscious meanings were being somatically expressed. This lack of clarity about how to understand herself kept reappearing in her therapy and undermining what I said or she said. There was a demand for me to locate 'the truth' and to give it to her. I think her preoccupation with the truth might have been linked to

Williams' ideas about being 'porous' to projections, with accompanying confusion about where projections were coming from and whose projections they were. Ellen herself projected her anxiety into her body, as was evidenced by the various illnesses she had been concerned about, some of which turned out to have a physiological basis, but others did not (such as cancer). Hamburg may be right in that bulimia kept Ellen sane until she could develop the capacity to develop other ways of defending herself against perceived danger, whether it came from inside or outside. Towards the end of her therapy, Ellen said she did not know what I had done to make a difference to her and that she was no longer concerned about it, but she felt as if channels in her mind that had been blocked were now free and she could think.

---

Some key points

- The meaning of bulimic symptoms may be discovered through enactment as well as by interpreting what the patient says.
- The transference may alternate.
- Nourishment will almost certainly be felt as poison.
- Intrusion and intimacy may be confused.
- Some bulimics may have a borderline personality disorder.
- Food, work, drink, sex, socialising, therapy may all be used bulimically.
- Bulimics can respond well (though intensely) to a psychoanalytic approach.
- Bulimia may be a defence against total breakdown.

# 5

# OBESITY

What is considered obese, or overweight, has fluctuated over time and geography. If we think about average weight as a guide we become confused as this has gradually crept up too, since 1959, when the Metropolitan Life Assurance Company of America established reference tables (Dally and Gomez, 1980: 27). The most commonly accepted way of deciding into which category a body falls is the Body Mass Index (BMI). The BMI is calculated by dividing one's weight in kilograms by height in metres squared. A BMI of less than 20 is underweight, 20–25 is normal, 25–30 is overweight and 30+ is considered obese. As mentioned earlier, the average statistics for Miss America have decreased over the last 30 years (see Garner *et al.*, 1980) as have the vital statistics of Playboy magazine centrefold models – there is no consistent 'ideal' weight or size. It is clear that lower weight is increasingly associated with greater beauty in women. Furthermore, this tendency is spread by exposure to Western media so that in parts of the world where low weight has not always been associated with physical attractiveness in women, it becomes so when television is introduced.*

Statistics are only data collected for a specific purpose – they tell us little about how the general tendency to put on weight at puberty and in middle age have become problematised or why some people get very big yet may still keep on eating. However, concern about body

---

* In 2002 Dr Anne Becker published a paper in the British Journal of Psychiatry about the influence of TV on the inhabitants of Fiji and its impact on the development of eating disorders amongst a population who had not seen TV before the mid-1990s. Eighty-three per cent of people felt TV had influenced their perceptions and thoughts about body image and size since its introduction.

size is prevalent even amongst children of both genders.** There are many different theories about why some people are fatter than others, such as genetic predisposition (Ravussin *et al.*, 1988; Roberts *et al.*, 1988) or glandular disorders such as Cushing's syndrome or Hypothyroidism which, in fact are uncommon, or lack of exercise or habituation since childhood to highly calorific foods. The last thing I would want to encourage is a belief that there is a 'normal' weight and that to be under or over this mythical line represents cause for concern. There is an engaging and refreshing website (www.adiosbarbie.com) for anyone who wants an antidote to attempts to create anxiety about eating and body shape.

It may be that obesity and compulsive eating relate to the same category of experience but with obesity describing the result, and compulsive eating the method by which the result is achieved. The term obesity feels pejorative to me but the term compulsive eating, doesn't quite convey the extent to which a result may affect someone's life. I am here considering the kind of relationship to food and eating which leaves a person feeling trapped in a way of relating to themselves and the world which is far removed from the sense of freedom to be whatever they wish, as is embraced in the website I have just mentioned. Clearly, I am also referring to an eating disorder with no link to an underlying physical causation.

There are, however, some physical consequences of eating compulsively other than weight gain (see Dally and Gomez, 1980). Obesity can predispose to diabetes mellitus and diseases of the heart and arteries and is linked to a shorter life span. Furthermore, joints can be put under strain when carrying a very heavy body. There is an increased risk of diverticular disease of the bowel and hiatus hernia at the upper end of the digestive tract. Fertility can be reduced in men and in women who may also suffer complications such as toxaemia and high blood pressure, if they do become pregnant. Both men and women are at greater risk during surgical operations and there is a greater incidence of gout and varicose veins amongst the obese. There can be a vicious cycle set up whereby exercise becomes too embarrassing and too uncomfortable so that physical problems are

---

** Also in 2002 the British Journal of Clinical Psychology published a paper 'Development of the children's body image scale' by Truby and Paxton. The paper records an extensive study into children's perceptions and expectations of their own body image. The authors found internalisation of a thin body ideal takes place at a young age with many children desiring a BMI below the average norm.

exacerbated by inactivity or the individual is put at risk by exercise itself. The ordinary, everyday symptoms of obesity include breathlessness, and mental, as well as physical lassitude. Psychologically, there can be depression and loss of confidence. However, these are general, psychological and physical symptoms associated with weight gain. What is of much more relevance is understanding the particular dynamics at work in the unconscious mind of someone who has become obese and feels unable to be any different.

## Psychotherapeutic encounters with patients who are obese

In order to explore some of the issues at stake in obesity I want to consider several psychoanalytic concepts used to understand obesity and then to describe in some detail the long-term therapy of a woman I shall call Amy. I learned a great deal from Amy and I value enormously her permission to include details about the work we did together, although I have, of course, disguised her identity and aspects of her therapy too, where necessary, so that she cannot be identified except by herself. This means that there is an element of fiction introduced into the account but I hope this clinical license will be tolerated and appreciated for what it is. However, before I set about describing a rewarding therapy from my own independent practice I, briefly, want to mention another patient with whom I had only a fleeting and very sad encounter. I will call this woman Fiona, and again, the details have been changed to protect her identity.

I met Fiona when I worked in a community mental health team as an Occupational Therapist. I was part of a crisis team, which operated in a large city and would visit patients in the community at the behest of their GP or hospital doctor with a view to an emergency admission to a psychiatric ward or a follow-up treatment in the community. Two consultant psychiatrists had clinical responsibility for the team. It was at about lunchtime that I was contacted by 'phone from a nurse in charge of a surgical ward in the local hospital. She told me they had a patient who was due to undergo an operation to clamp her stomach and that she had been on bed-rest for some time while the nursing staff attempted to help her reduce her food intake sufficiently so that she could lose a little weight in order to have the operation which would help her lose a lot of weight. The patient had not co-operated and they could not operate. The nursing staff needed the bed and the patient was distressed. As the patient had an eating disorder, perhaps there was some help available from the community mental health team or from psychiatry? I went along to the ward and saw the patient immediately as I entered. She could not be missed – she was in a special large bed and, literally, was flowing over the sides of it.

I sat and talked to her, asking about the background to her current situation and trying to assess whether or not there was a justifiable reason to admit this person to a psychiatric bed, though as we talked, I realised that there would be no bed big enough in the whole of the psychiatric unit. Fiona was a pleasant and talkative young woman, in her twenties, with no apparent concern for her plight. She told me that she had fallen out with the nurses and that they didn't like her because she was fat. She had been waiting for some time to have the operation because she could not diet and could no longer walk. She could not even stand to have a shower and her home had been adapted specially to permit her to survive in this disabled condition. She could teeter around between the bed, the shower chair and the toilet and was completely dependent on an older man who was like a surrogate father who took care of her. It was not possible to dip below the surface of this description of her life – Fiona was blithe and expressed no feelings of depression though she seemed to agree that she was in a difficult situation and said she wanted some help.

It is a long time ago since I met Fiona and time has blurred many of the details of our encounter but it has not dulled what I remember now as I write in terms of my own emotional response. We therapists can talk about countertransference or affective responses to our patients and it can seem very professional and expert. What I remember, though, is better described by a much more colourful and vulgar expression: I felt absolutely gutted. While Fiona talked blithely and I made a big effort not to show how shocked and helpless I felt at the sight of her, something terribly sad gripped me and made me want to find a way of rescuing her. I had, at this point in my career, already begun training as a psychotherapist and was sometimes aware of rescue fantasies alerting me to a potential projective identification in which I might be getting entangled. I left the patient to consult with my colleagues who agreed that the patient should be seen at home by a member of our team and given some support in her resumption of a diet in order to get to a weight where surgery was possible. I knew I was about to leave for another job and wondered who would be willing to take on such a task. Meanwhile I was asked to see Fiona at home.

Depressing as it was in the hospital, seeing Fiona at home was even more disheartening. Fiona lived in one room with the shower room and toilet leading off. There were no carpets or furniture other than a big bed and a chest of drawers and one or two chairs. The door was on the latch so that she didn't have to get up to open it and neighbourhood children, a dog and the surrogate father came and went. This might sound sociable but there was an air of casual neglect and lack of concern about privacy and safety. Fiona was also worried about teenage boys on the estate taking advantage of her. Fiona showed me her stock of snacks – six packets of crisps. She could not give them up – this was all she liked eating. However, her pride and joy was a Citizen's Band (CB) radio sitting on the chest of drawers next to the bed. She demonstrated how she made contact with her friends and regaled me with entertaining stories. She was pleased I would visit but I was unable to have anything other than a social conversation with her as people came and went. I was more than dismayed about how I would make any in roads into this 'belle indifférence'.***

The next week when I visited I was told that she had a new appointment to be admitted shortly to hospital again (though she hadn't lost any weight) and so my involvement came to an end. I left the job some weeks later and heard nothing about Fiona until three years later. A former colleague rang me and told me 'my' patient had been admitted to hospital. My colleague wanted to know what to do about liaising with me. At first, I had no idea what she was talking about, as the patient's name had slipped from my memory. However, when Fiona was described (still extremely obese) she came straight back to mind and I was flabbergasted that she had told her psychiatrist that I had been seeing her for three years! Whether this was simply a lie, or a way of recalling me back into her life, I will never know. The reason I am mentioning Fiona here is that her situation and the role that I played convince me that there are some very important ways in which good listening and counselling skills from a range of professional helpers who are not formally trained in psychotherapeutic skills should not be underestimated. Thoughtful people who can listen and a take a humane approach can save lives and help get a person to a state where they can accept more formal, change-orientated psychotherapy. Fiona had kept me in her mind for three years, perhaps holding onto a possibility that there could be someone who could help her one day. It is to an account of a more formal twice-a-week psychoanalytic psychotherapy that I want to turn

*** This is a term normally reserved for people who are psychotic and yet it seems the best way of describing Fiona's total lack of anxiety about her predicament.

in order to be able to examine more closely what might be at issue but first I want to map out some basic psychoanalytic theory.

## The psychodynamics of obesity

There is much less written about obesity and compulsive eating than there is about anorexia and bulimia in the psychoanalytic literature. This may, in part, be due to the belief that there is an organic component. As Thorner commented: 'Obesity is undoubtedly a complex disorder. A few cases are of purely organic origin but the majority of cases are a complex personality reaction in which overeating is only one factor, lack of energy output another in addition to some unknown constitutional factor' (1970: 321). Sometimes there is a purely organic aetiology to obesity. The ICD-10 puts obesity in the category of endocrinal, nutritional and metabolic disease whereas anorexia and bulimia are firmly in the category of mental and behavioural disorders.

Castelnuoveo-Tedesco and Whisnant Reiser (1988) suggested that people who are obese do not readily seek treatment and when they do it is for a direct approach to the symptom rather than the more comprehensive approach of psychoanalysis. This may be one reason that the literature about working with the obese psychoanalytically is relatively small. Rand and Stunkard (cited in the same paper) surveyed 84 obese patients who had been treated analytically and found only 6 per cent had presented with a chief complaint of obesity.

Thorner observed that obese people who had sought his help had very disturbed object relations: they hated their own bodies and were depressed and felt persecuted and rejected by the outside world. He viewed the way in which their inner world operated as being akin to the relation between the baby and the breast. The baby gets support and relief from being fed and feels secure and satisfied. This link between a good feed and a good object or parent who feeds, is the basic template for relating and being. However, the obese person's sense of satisfaction is short-lived because she then feels 'the breast' is exhausted and damaged and this leads to an increase in anxiety which makes her need to reassure herself by another feed. This compulsion to repeat the feeding situation creates a vicious circle. What might look like greed is, to some extent, a compulsion. Thorner wondered why such patients show signs that they cannot tolerate the normal interruptions inherent in feeding. The more the baby can feel love for the breast and gratitude for the feed, the more able she is to cope with the separation from it and to believe that she has not exhausted or damaged it. If the baby hates or envies the breast then the more likely the baby will feel it has destroyed the breast. Thorner's use of the Kleinian idea of primary envy is not the only way to understand this scenario. If the baby cannot control the coming and going of the breast there is a basic and unavoidable threat to its sense of omnipotence. Some babies might just want more than they get or cannot tolerate the frustration they feel when the breast doesn't come to them just when they wish it. Whatever the underlying phantasy about the object which can satisfy or frustrate, there is a problem with accepting the rhythm of the feeding pattern in people who feed compulsively. An insecure, anxious baby who doesn't understand where the breast has gone cannot feel gratitude and might feel persecuted. What is taken in then becomes a damaging/damaged object. The obese person feels full of bad hateful things and projects hate into her body, especially any parts such as the breasts and the stomach, which are linked to mother in her mind.

Eating thus becomes linked to self-regulation in terms of anxiety and hate, as well as hunger. The oral zone remains extremely important and in the obese person's psychosexual development holds precedence over the genital zone for satisfaction and also confers a similar lack of stable satisfaction on any consequent development. Bruch summed up the range of possibilities expressed by our relationship to food:

> Food may symbolically stand for an insatiable desire for unobtainable love, or expression of rage and hatred; it may substitute for sexual gratification or indicate ascetic denial; it may represent the wish to be a man and possess a penis, or the wish to be pregnant, or fear of it. Food may help one achieve a sense of spurious power and self-aggrandizement, or serve as a defense against adulthood and responsibility. Preoccupation with food may appear as helpless dependent clinging to parents, or as a hostile rejection of them. (Bruch, 1969: 130–1)

However, the main reason for seeking psychotherapy may well not be an eating disorder or simply dissatisfaction with the body, often people have become depressed and feel somewhat at the mercy of the world around them, perhaps to the extent of being paranoid. Thorner questioned whether or not the change in the body image in several patients he saw was linked to anxieties of a psychotic kind and cautioned against prematurely exposing the patient who eats compulsively to the psychosis against which obesity may be a defence.

He quoted from Hilda Bruch: 'obesity … is a symptom and not a disease and can not and should not be removed until the underlying disturbances are corrected' (1957: 402).

The oral phase as the fixation point in the development of obesity was traditionally the main focus of attention by psychoanalysts since Freud developed the idea of the mouth as a principal erotogenic zone (1905: 179–84) and Alexander (1934) linked obesity to a disturbance in it. In short, the idea was that too little or too much gratification at this stage created a kind of 'hot' spot beyond which further sound development was hampered. Under stress, the person may regress to oral satisfactions such as smoking, thumb-sucking, drinking and, of course, eating. This earlier period of their lives having also given them some sense of security as well as pleasure which, under duress, can be recaptured, albeit in a more or less pathological way. The yearning for someone to help contain a feeling gets crossed with the concrete feeding experience so that food comes not only to represent mother but also to be a kind of controllable alternative to a person. Most children consciously separate mother from food by the age of two, according to Anna Freud (1972), but an unconscious connection remains. In eating-disordered people this seems to be in the realm of a symbolic equation along the lines of food = mother rather than an association (see Segal [1978] to understand better the differences Segal perceives between a true symbol and a symbolic equation). What may be most significant to those working with obese patients is that a symbolic representation can only be created where a loss has been felt. If separation or loss is denied, or disavowed, there can be no true symbol formation, an equation is made instead. Whether this means that the loss of a mother has been avoided or the very idea of a loss outside of the control of the individual, the idea of separation itself, is held at bay, is worthy of further consideration and we will return to it at a later point when exploring the concept of psychic retreats as developed by Steiner (1993).

Grinberg (1956) emphasised the role of negation in obesity. The obese person denies having lost or destroyed the object and maintains a continuous relation with its substitute – food. As Grinberg put it: 'It is not true that the object is gone; I did not destroy it. The proof of this is that I see it bodily before me; I can always find it and ingest it; so it must be here' (p.167). The negation requires food to be available at any time – there is an addictive quality to the repetition required. Grinberg noticed that obese people might also be addicted to certain people in their life too.

Bruch (1957) argued that the mothers of people who become obese may have offered food instead of some other response to their

children when they have expressed a need. This may be due to difficulties of their own, which have prevented them from either being
appropriately attuned or capable of a range of other responses but
the upshot is that the child does not then read his or her own internal
state accurately and cannot respond to it in a variety of ways. Instead,
the child turns to food when his or her internal state is affected by
strong feelings and, importantly, by hunger. The differences between
feeling hungry, abandoned, attacked, hated or lonely then lose
meaning – the obese person cannot bear their hunger, imbued as it is
with so many feeling states and unacknowledged limitations and
phantasies. As Bruch suggested:

> Failure to obtain a regular and persistent response appropriate to
> his needs deprives the developing child of the essential ground-
> work for his 'body identity' and perceptual and conceptual
> awareness of his own functions. A child growing up this way may
> acquire the facade of adequate functioning by robot-like co-operation
> with environmental demands. The gross deficit in initiative and
> active self-expression will become manifest when he is confronted
> with new situations, such as going to camp or college, or at puberty
> with its new demands for which the distorted routine of his
> background has left him unprepared. Such an individual may feel
> helpless under the impact of his bodily urges, or feel controlled
> from the outside, as if he did not own his body. (Bruch, 1969: 137)

The American self psychologists put it another way: the obese person
lacks the capacity to self-soothe because they have suffered a failure
of empathic mirroring in childhood and have not acquired the internal capacities that ensue and would normally strengthen the ego and
its representational functions (see Goodsitt, 1983). Some writers have
concluded that overeating can be seen as a form of self-medication
(Glucksman, 1989).

Another aspect of obesity is the effect on self-image of the body
representation and vice-versa. Post (Castelnuoveo-Tedesco and
Whisnant Reiser, 1988: 168) did not find fear of being fat in the obese
but rather a fear of being thin – though what thin means to a person
differs. Glucksman and Hirsch (1969) found that obese patients had
trouble estimating their body size and tend to overestimate it. Bruch
thought that obese children might need to exaggerate their size in
response to feelings of emptiness or vulnerability or to compensate
their parents who they might feel are disappointed with them. Once
someone has become obese, there are plenty of societal cues to

encourage or reinforce self-loathing. Glucksman researched obesity extensively from a psychodynamic perspective and has written about a particular patient he saw for 14 years and who was a research subject. His patient's weight fluctuated throughout the treatment and though he seemed to have worked consistently psychoanalytically, his final conclusions are very circumscribed:

> ... although therapy can be effective in promoting positive changes in self and body-image for obese patients, it may not be as effective in bringing about a permanently lowered body weight ... Although hyperphagia and weight fluctuations definitely articulate with psychodynamic processes, there are underlying genetic, metabolic, morphologic and neurochemical phenomena that exert profound influence on body weight over an extended period of time. Similar to other psychophysiological disorders, obesity appears to be the final common pathway resulting from a complex interaction between critical developmental experiences and genetically determined biological processes. (Glucksman, 1989: 168–9)

Although I only saw Amy for half the period that Glucksman saw his patient, I have felt rather more optimistic, though there are some distinct differences, which may have been beneficial to my patient. One important difference was that, at our first meeting, my patient presented several different concerns and her weight was not the only leading concern. Furthermore, I admitted I did not know if the therapy would help her reduce her weight or not and that I felt it was her responsibility to lose the weight if she wanted to. I was also able to see Amy twice a week, and this may have been more frequent than Glucksman's therapy. I was also building on six years of work carried out earlier by a previous analytic therapist.

## Amy: an introduction to a clinical case

Amy was a high-flying product developer for a large company in the south of England and had just been relocated to a senior position in the northern headquarters of this company, based in a neighbouring city. She was a large, imposing woman in her late thirties, dressed in a plain, rather drab way, as if she had no interest in how she looked. However, her eyes were bright and she wore her hair in a stylish cut and she had an impish smile. She was worried about her weight which had crept up again since she had left her previous therapist some years ago and felt she needed some support in losing it. She felt isolated in her new post – there were no other women in the north who she could see as equal colleagues and she missed the company of the people she had left behind, especially her female partner of several years standing. She wasn't sure she would stay in the north as her partner refused to move and travelling to see her at weekends was so exhausting.

Amy's career had begun to blossom in the last two years and she had been able to design and develop new products, with the help of colleagues, which could prove to be both beneficial to many people and also highly profitable. However, she found herself unable to draw a line around who should be included in the list of designers/ inventors and who should be left out. It was hard to decide both practically and morally. Indeed, she told me, she found it hard, in general to tell right from wrong. Her inclination was to include everyone in the list of contributors as this would cause fewer problems. However, some of her co-designers were indignant about her over inclusiveness.

Amy had also been involved in voluntary work for a charity, which helped people with long-term mental health problems and had recently been in contact with a client who cross-dressed. She had since experienced intrusive thoughts when she was attending project meetings in other regions: people might think she was a man dressed as a woman.

Amy had been interested in working in the field of mental health when she was younger and had gone into therapy herself, recognising that she had some difficulties of her own. These included a string of sexual relationships with older women who had power over her, even though she was not sexually attracted to them, low self-esteem and weight gain. She had thrived during the six years of therapy and had not understood why it had been terminated, although she agreed to it herself and acknowledged that she had lost a lot of weight. She had changed her mind about a career in mental health and resumed the career in which she seemed ably qualified and talented.

## Amy's therapy

In a long, twice-a-week, psychoanalytic psychotherapy, it is impossible to condense the work into a few pages: there are bound to be distortions. For the sake of simplicity, I will divide the therapy into three phases: the settling in phase; the central phase of discovering the patient's inner world and, its effects on the transference and countertransference; and the final phase of integrating change and ending.

The first phase of therapy was linked to the assessment (see Chapter 6 for further details) which I had decided to approach as a trial period of therapy. This was partly because I wasn't sure if she would stay in the north and also I was unsure if she could work with me. Looking back now, it seems I encountered a rather contemptuous woman and my doubts seem well founded. Amy was quite forthright, very chatty and not shy about asking personal questions. She asked how old was my house and thought it was nearly as nice as the house of her previous therapist; she asked if I could get her some tea; she puzzled over why I charged less than her previous therapist and offered to pay more; was I training still, she wondered; and did I mind the fact that she had a better paid job than mine? She was taken aback when I interpreted some of her comments, especially her envy of what she thought I had that she lacked, despite the denigratory comments. Indeed, for the first few years of her therapy Amy resisted strongly my attempts to link what she said to the transference. There was one exception to this general tendency and that was when I made interpretations about boundaries and her fears that I wouldn't know right from wrong and that she couldn't always tell either. She constantly overstepped the mark about boundaries herself, not only in her comments but also by cancelling sessions and forgetting to pay but her unconscious anxieties about boundaries being intruded upon went much deeper. She would sleep with a 'phone next to her bed at night and worry about a man breaking in and attacking her. She also thought the creaky noises my house made when the central heating went on or off, could be a man skulking in the corridor and she would break off from what she was saying to listen out. When I tried to address other 'here and now' issues in the transference, at first she expressed polite interest laced with scepticism but eventually, making transference interpretations became a risky business and it would enrage her. She didn't mind me making interpretations about her childhood and past events ('there and then' interpretations), but she fought against, what in her mind, seemed to be me trying constantly to bring myself in and get attention. 'Look!' she would say, 'this isn't about you!' She used the full extent of her considerable intellect to show me how misguided my approach was – she explicitly asked that I should, instead, for example, give her guidelines for how she should tackle mounting interpersonal problems with her colleagues. Making transference interpretations that could be used was a challenge to my ingenuity and, I must confess, I sometimes had to employ my sense of humour, which is a chancy affair, too.

Nonetheless, Amy stayed and the story of her upbringing and past history was elaborated and brought to life in her relationship with me and the world around her. She was a middle child, with an attractive older sister who was considered 'weak' and therefore rather despicable in her mother's eyes and in Amy's view. However, this daughter seemed to have won approval from Amy's father who responded tenderly to his daughter when she was upset. Amy felt that father was scornful of her own person especially because he did not find her 'pleasing' physically and he was not interested in her achievements and inventions. Furthermore, he was on the periphery of the family anyway, according to Amy. There were also younger twin brothers whose personalities were hardly discernible in what Amy said about them in the first few years of therapy, and who seemed slightly estranged from the family. Amy described her mother as attentive but only in order to win acclaim for herself and to bask in any successes of Amy's. Mother was a large, dominant, woman too, who used Amy as a confidante, expressing great interest in her sexuality. Indeed, both parents were, according to Amy, 'unfazed' by her accounts of sexual relationships with much older women who were in positions of responsibility for the welfare of their daughter. Amy herself thought she had seduced and used these women. Amy felt she was the apple of her mother's eye but only because mother was so needy and unhappy in her own marriage and regarded her daughter's visits as an opportunity to talk about herself and be gratified.

Amy remembered an event in childhood, which seemed to represent not only the background to tensions within the family, but also painted a vivid picture of her own internal objects. Amy mentioned several times that she had come home from school once to find her mother had written a letter to the local children's home and put it in an addressed envelope which was placed on the mantelpiece. Mother lined up the children and told them that she would send this letter asking for the children to be taken into care if they did not behave themselves. She couldn't cope with them anymore and they had to be more grown up. Amy's sister broke down and cried, her brothers didn't understand and Amy vowed to herself that she would never ever let anyone reduce her to tears and that she would not be sent away. From that day on she set about making sure she did what she believed her mother wished in order to avoid a catastrophe. However, she 'put away childish things' so to speak when she was only seven years old! Since then she had never cried, knew how to manage her mother, did well at school and took care of the house and herself when her mother went off to work at night. She would go out to play and peer in through the windows at other families eating their supper together. At home she ate sandwiches she made herself and ironed and cleaned before her mother came home from work. To her great shame, she was also cruel to her brothers who were toddlers. Internally, she identified with an aggressor, suppressed the vulnerable her and despised any sign of weakness wherever she saw it. Yet something had not hardened completely, because she was capable of sympathy and support for people who were very vulnerable – the mentally ill. By taking care of them she got some vicarious caring, and importantly, was able to project her needy, vulnerable self, into them. However, Amy also recalled that before this episode, when her mother had returned with her newborn twins from hospital, something had already changed in her mother. She learned later of a puerperal breakdown that had occurred but, at the time, what she felt was that her mother had been replaced by a robot – a woman who did things like her mother had, but mechanically and without feeling. Yet, she could not remember the time before this happened or the non-robotic mother and suffered a kind of early childhood amnesia.

Amy's adolescence was marked by an absence of sexual experimentation and an emphasis on schoolwork and sport. She was acutely aware of her older sister's attractiveness and popularity and may have wanted to avoid competition with her. She did well academically and went off to college. While a student, she became involved sexually with several older women, although she seems to have been motivated more by the wish for comfort and security than sex or love. At around the same time she noticed another student who was obese and observed her from a distance. She found this woman repulsive and was struck by the idea that she too would like to look the same. She began to put on weight. As well as getting bigger, and perhaps projecting her self-loathing into her body, and maybe anaesthetising herself sexually too, Amy could let a more infantile her appreciate the affection and security she had found in intimate relationships. She discovered 'caring' and decided to work in mental health and went into therapy herself. This allowed her to feel understood but she maintained that it was always a very cerebral business. I wonder if that was the only access the therapist was allowed to have and that Amy kept him both at a distance, and on a terrain which was unthreatening to her. She found the therapy stimulating and also lost weight. She agreed to ending but secretly felt she had been dropped just as she was getting more confident and had begun to explore heterosexual feelings (which may have been directed to her male therapist).

During the first phase of her therapy, Amy became accustomed again to having someone reliable to talk to who would try to understand her from a psychoanalytic perspective, linking the past and the present through the transference. Although she constantly denied links in the transference, she settled into the weekly routine, although cancelled sessions sometimes because of work commitments. She tended to treat me somewhat as she herself had been treated: I would be dropped in favour of something else; I would be listened to but often felt that what she wanted was to have my attention and support; and she was less able to take on board what I said if it challenged her need for security or comfort. Even so, she was in a relationship with me, seeing me as like her sister – 'touchy-feely' and weak, though basically benign, while she was strong. She was afraid she would discover that I was vulnerable and would be upset about the things she told me and that I wanted to turn her into a weak person like her sister. This gradually altered in that the concept 'weak' became more complex: she was afraid I would make her messy and disorganised too. She was terrified I would turn her into an ordinary feeling human being and then she wouldn't be able to function.

The corollary to the creation of a precocious caretaker self which had helped her since she was seven, was a sense of being fake in other areas too. Though clearly talented, she was always anxious about being exposed as a fraud in her job. She felt she had always been acting and so did not genuinely possess talent, intelligence or empathy for others. Amy also felt guilty about any successes she had, believing they were always at someone else's expense. During this phase too, there emerged a fear that she had been sexually abused as a child and there was plenty of material which suggested a very sexualised atmosphere in the home in which she grew up – both in terms of her father's voyeuristic interest in other women and her mother's interest in her. It was difficult to know what was at stake but it was in keeping with a feeling she had that she could be either intruded upon in an intimate way by what was said or seen or that she could be drawn into something which made her feel disgusted and impinged upon. The actual examples she gave of incidents, which came to her mind, were always ambiguous. I began to see what she was telling me as related above all to the state of mind she was in, where contact of an emotional kind could feel sexualised or threatening so that she was left quite muddled about what was happening and what she wanted herself. At this point her own wish to really intrude into me and get into a mix-up with me became clear. I would try to pick up on her confused feelings about it, despite her objections to me putting myself in the picture.

After this first phase, she came to appreciate an opportunity to have someone all to herself for at least two hours a week, even though she seemed to believe I needed her rather then she needed me. However, her isolation both at work and socially, was becoming apparent. She began to describe problematic situations with colleagues and junior staff. Moreover, some six months after having started therapy, her mother became very ill and died. This was a very sad period in which, for the only time during her therapy, I saw Amy cry. Despite the difficulties in the family, there was much love between all of them and Amy's father, not so far distinguished by any great empathy according to Amy, managed, at the last moment, to support his dying wife and to release his children from the responsibility of coping with the very last moments of her life. After the bereavement, though, was another matter. Amy's father, in a kind of manic reaction (or so it seemed from Amy's description), threw himself into a series of ill-advised ventures as if to eradicate the experience of loss. This was a great strain on Amy, who found it hard to believe she had lost the mother she never fully felt she'd had in the first place. She imagined her mother's presence at home and even in my consulting room, and went through a stage of identification with her in illness, believing she was terminally ill. This happened at several anniversaries. The first long break was painful for Amy – she had thoughts about killing herself but denied it was anything to do with my absence and as subsequent breaks approached always denied she found them difficult, believing that I wanted her to miss me because I was insecure and narcissistic. She would also cancel sessions shortly after returning from a break from my holiday, as if she could not bear to be the one who was left and had to leave me too.

## Psychic retreats

The main thrust of the central part of Amy's therapy was related to what John Steiner called a 'psychic retreat' (1993) which describes aptly the mental state that had helped Amy throughout her life. Since childhood, she had literally taken herself off at times, I presume, to regulate herself internally when emotion threatened to burst through her self-holding. This habit had evolved further so that she had created a veritable 'other place' where her wishes could be satisfied in a magical way. What this involved, and it took place frequently, often when she was lonely or anxious or bored, was that she would take herself somewhere to buy chocolate and a soft drink. Then she would eat and drink while fantasising about being the centre of attention as awed admirers looked on and she performed as a musician or demonstrated some wonderful machine she had invented. As a matter of fact she could play the instrument concerned and had designed some less fantastic piece of technology. As we explored these more hidden sides of her life, Amy's projects at work began to attract some attention. She then seemed to enter even deeper into this private world of fantasy. She stopped seeing her friends when she visited her partner, made no efforts to socialise in her new workplace, dropped her voluntary work and simply worked inordinately long hours on her projects, and fantasised. She stopped taking off time at the weekends and didn't want to go away on holiday. She also put on a lot more weight. As I tried to take up with her what she was doing to herself, it was as if the omnipotence tied up in her psychic retreat and in her dreams took over more of her waking life. She began to get into ferocious arguments with a collaborator and was tempted to take him to court over a disagreement about their joint product. Amy felt bullied and was excited by this – she consciously admired her bully and wanted to be like him. She became aggressive with me too when I tried to bring the underlying issues into the transference. She harangued me for the way I worked and disputed that it was meant to be helpful for her – she had come to the conclusion that I was just like her mother and would do anything to get to talk about me.

This went on for a long time. She had also been amassing unpaid bills and was getting into a financial crisis. She kept forgetting to pay me and would get muddled up about whether she had paid or not and sometimes I got in a muddle too, as a kind of enactment took place where I really did become temporarily a bit disorganised about my fees. All the while there was a powerful mind at work, talking to me, with hardly any silences, arguing and demanding I explain to her what I must know about what she should do to handle situations better.

She was also becoming vindictive, wanting to hurt colleagues who she felt were cloying, calling me a 'benign bungler' and generally, behaving in an overbearing way with everyone including me. I kept trying to pick up both the defensive nature of what she did and the attack she was making on me and the her, who wanted to change. This went on and was particularly virulent when she had any career successes, which resulted in increased self-denigration. My comments about how she attacked herself at such times were immediately helpful and seemed to relieve her. The alternative to attacking herself was that she grew very grandiose after successes too – she was the everlasting bountiful breast. Paradoxically, she was also extremely paranoid about some colleagues and again, interpretation of these negative, frightening thoughts helped contain her, although it brought out her own destructiveness and wish to steal and benefit from other people without acknowledging them.

I came to the conclusion that part of her absolutely hated reality and the fact that she could not control what happened in it – even pleasant surprises were disturbing. Her turn to a psychic retreat had once been understandable but now it was a way of getting a kind of perverse excitement too when she knew she did have an alternative before her. The work was not easy and obviously there were many other things that happened along the way. We were both fortunate in that she discovered she could trust an older male colleague who became like a father to her. This seemed linked to the way that I had been able to continue to gain sustenance from my psychoanalytic family of ideas and to keep using psychoanalysis to bring in a perspective on me and her that helped to open up a space for emotional thinking. This kind of space, is linked according to Britton (1989) with the early Oedipal situation. A triangular space is created when one can tolerate knowing about a mother and a father who are a sexual partnership, from which one is excluded. The Oedipus complex is painful for us all but it gives us the freedom and perspective of thought which comes from facing up to one's limitations and place in the world.

## Integrating change

As she emerged from the psychic retreat, she was hyperaware of all couples, and of feelings of exclusions. Conscious envy and jealousy became possible. She became very concerned about how she looked and decided that as she no longer retreated to her fantasy world and her work did not require quite as much input as before, she needed to find some way of filling her time. She was angry that I had 'taken' her fantasy world away from her and said it was my fault she felt so bereft. She would ask plaintively what other people did who weren't like her. She gradually found some friends and some interests outside of work, including re-discovering her love of sport. Slowly she began to include some exercise into her routine and began to cook for herself. She moved house several times until she got nearer to something she could afford but which gave her the possibility of having people over to eat with her.

Amy also decided to start to lose weight and I was encouraged by her wish to look after herself, while neither helping with, nor distancing myself from, her diet. Amy was helped more specifically by a thoughtful GP and a dietician who advised her and supported her. She was also prescribed medication, which made her feel ill, if she ate fat. At the end of seven years, she was a greatly changed person internally. She was touched when I was sympathetic to her when she had been ill and began to express gratitude for the help she had been given. She no longer felt that if I interpreted her need of me that I was trying to get something for myself that I didn't deserve. She also began to be aware of other peoples' sexual attractiveness and how powerful an advantage this was for them and how unfair it is for those of us who are not blessed with great beauty. She got jealous of a colleague and was inclined to try to spoil her career but recovered her equilibrium without making an attack, other than privately, in words to me. Amy overstepped a boundary of appropriate behaviour with her partner and was rebuked and became able to see how this, too, had been motivated by her own jealousy. What was most surprising was the way she even made some transference interpretations herself!

I tried to pick up the parallels between the ending in her previous therapy and the ending we faced, especially a secret and unacknowledged wish to feel she could seduce me. Only time will tell if the work we did will hold and whether or not her destructiveness will get the upper hand when she suffers the normal slings and arrows of misfortune. When she began to feel that she could leave the therapy, a new phase opened up, as she put in place a series of celebrations – some large, like reunions and parties, some small, like buying brighter, more youthful clothes. I was left feeling reasonably optimistic. By the time we finished, she had lost nine stone and hoped to lose a little more. She had no plans to become thin.

## Discussion

The account of Amy's therapy demonstrates that many of the underlying issues mentioned by researchers and writers in the field seem to feature strongly. Amy's very early experiences were lost from her memory but as the therapy progressed fragments of good memories of her mother and much stronger positive memories of her father began to appear. However, there did seem to have been a breakdown in a containing relationship with both mother and father from the age of seven. We cannot know what kind of real experience Amy had before that, in the pre-oedipal, pre-verbal period when one imagines her particular relationship with food was founded. Amy seemed to suffer a deterioration in her relationships from the age of seven but we must also bear in mind that at seven she was also coming to terms with both the return of a mother who had gone off to have her babies, and two more rivals for both parents' attention to deal with. Amy may well have been disturbed by both these aspects as well as by finding herself, in her mind and perhaps literally too, left to her own devices in terms of growing up and taking care of herself.

Amy tended to use eating as a way of managing herself when she was stirred up by anger or jealousy or loneliness and particularly by depression and paranoid feelings as Grinberg so poignantly described (1992: 140–51). Indeed, any strong feeling or in new situations, she had discovered a way of never feeling deprived and which also intensified her sense of omnipotence and the phantasy that she couldn't be deprived – she had it all and could bestow her favours on others. Indeed, her worry that people might believe she was a man dressed as a woman may have expressed a conviction that she really did have it all, including an all powerful penis – the phallus represented as the musical instrument others admired or the impressive bit of kit in her fantasy! This concern disappeared very quickly as the dynamics involved in its creation moved into the transference.

The use of eating to mask her deprivations and inner feelings of emptiness fit with the picture painted by Bruch, Glucksman, Grinsberg and Thorner and others. However real Amy's deficits were or were felt to be, there was also a use of eating and the fantasies associated with it, to create a psychic retreat which became a way of rejecting change or development. Furthermore, a perverse pleasure and addictive excitement could be gained from what included not only a kind of oral masturbation, but also a hateful attack on her objects, including me, in the transference. This is an aspect of eating disorders, which is tricky to get at: not only the depression, but the paranoia and the hate wrapped up in a self-preservative package. Like Bruch (see above p. 76), I think it can be damaging to the patient for the symptom of obesity to be treated as a cause of disturbance – it really can combine some enormously difficult developmental problems with some very destructive impulses in certain people. Hate, envy and jealousy are particularly hard to deal with when there has been insufficient containment due to either failure in parenting or excessive demands made by a child. However, another important feature is related to orality itself. Freud thought that what he called the component sexual instincts did not fuse together satisfactorily until we matured and were able to enjoy genital sexuality with a partner. Where a person is fixated at an oral stage, it would seem that hate has not been adequately bound to love and this leaves the individual at the mercy of some very strong feelings. Hunger feels dangerous. Hate feels dangerous. And I think this means that love, too must feel dangerous when there has been a difficulty in believing in a good parental couple who can love each other and their child.

Some key points

- Models based on developmental deficit are helpful but they may obscure active processes going on in the here and now.
- Interpretation of transference in a sensitive way can be effective, despite resistance to it.
- The patient's depression, paranoia and hate need to be held in mind.
- Suicidality is possible when the patient becomes more able to experience loss.
- Working through, particularly in relation to the lost or destroyed object, needs a long time and denial can be a stumbling block.
- Creating a space to think emotionally involves addressing pre-oedipal and Oedipal issues.
- The work of helping someone give up a psychic retreat is slow and the therapist should expect to feel stuck.
- Weight loss is the business of the patient – the therapist should beware buying into the idea that the patient's size has to be tackled. However, the way the patient relates to food and hunger should be addressed, but avoiding a judgmental attitude about size.
- The patients self-care and relations with her internal and external objects are a better focus of intervention.
- Patients may need more than one shot at therapy in their lives.

# 6

# ISSUES FOR THE PRACTITIONER

## Introduction

This chapter will bring together some of the issues that have emerged from the discussion of eating disorders so far, and also some further areas, which remain outstanding, and which affect the thinking and practice of clinicians. The first issue is assessment. This is a big question because many eating-disordered people turn down the offer of help, either by not attending an assessment or not taking up a referral for psychotherapy or counselling after the assessment. Liaison and management are also especially important, as there can sometimes be a significant threat to life by starvation and suicide attempts as well as the physical consequences of some forms of eating disorder. After a short section looking at these areas I go on to reconsider briefly the challenges to practise that have been highlighted by some authoritative experts like Hilde Bruch as well as others, and then discuss them in relation to transference and countertransference, revisiting ideas about how change comes about in our work. I then take a perspective on the problematic question of body image disturbance, which has been researched extensively in relation to anorexia, in particular. This leads on to another brief discussion about men and eating disorders, this time, in relation to gender and sexuality. Finally, I finish with a short section on supervision.

## Assessment

The orientation of this book is basically psychoanalytic although the work described is once or twice-a-week psychotherapy. Others (Birksted-Breen, 1989; Flanders, 2001; Lawrence, 2002) have given an account of the work they have carried out with patients at a more intensive frequency. In public sector psychotherapy services and student counselling centres, it is quite unusual to work at such an intense frequency and it is in such places that most people with an eating disorder are seen. When it comes to assessing patients for psychotherapy and counselling, the question of how much the patient can use or bear is uppermost, whether it is about frequency or interpretation. As in all assessments for psychotherapy, it is crucial to keep in mind that the meeting may be the first time a person has an experience of being truly listened to and thought about, and this can be both a relief and very disturbing. As mentioned several times, people with eating disorders may feel very lonely and depressed, and need to feel controlled over eating is not being wrestled away from them, and that they and their body are not unacceptable. Adolescents who are assessed may need a modified approach and very careful handling since an eating disorder is linked to a key issue of adolescence: acceptance and integration of the developing sexual body. The level of disturbance expressed by an eating disorder may not be apparent at first encounter (see Laufer and Laufer, 1984 for an illuminating discussion of assessment of adolescents).

The general literature on eating disorders (Bruch, 1970; Crisp, 1980; Dally, 1980) often suggests that adopting a psychoanalytic stance does not help, especially when the patient is an anorexic at low weight. This may be felt to be especially true at assessment, when the therapist is under some strain and the habitual approach seems to meet with resistance. Many psychotherapists like to give trial interpretations in their assessment meeting to gauge whether or not the patient is able to work with them in an analytic way. Sometimes this is not advisable, as with some anorexic patients, for example. However, not all psychoanalytically orientated practitioners would attempt an interpretation at first meeting. Jane Milton has depicted two quite opposite styles of assessment, one more intrusive than the other and akin to a medical investigation that opens up the patient (Milton, 1997). However, not all psychoanalysts favour the more 'surgical' style and like to establish a therapeutic alliance before risking an interpretation. I have found the latter approach to be the most helpful with anorexic patients as is a sense of a shared effort to explore whether or not psychotherapy might be of benefit.

It may be that an assessment needs to take place over several different sessions for there to be an experience of being listened to and understood correctly, and to enable the patient to allow some emotional contact. Williams (1997) recommends that whoever assesses should be the person who carries on seeing the patient. In the clinical examples I gave, my anorexic patient, Jenny, was very 'wrapped up' at assessment, and I had to find a language we could use together to begin to unpackage her inner world. Williams talks of using 'pastel colours' not 'primary colours' in her language, and I similarly, employed the suffix 'ish' when mentioning delicate matters like her mood or what she ate. Another patient who was anorexic came very late to her first session and described how she had been in a traffic jam. I made an interpretation about this and how little time she had left for herself and as a consequence what a jam her mind might be in. This was too much too soon for this patient and she did not return. Some anorexic patients come to their first assessment session and hardly speak at all. The therapist can feel compelled to ask questions which, of course, will be felt to be unhelpful and will get nowhere. Yet silence is intimidating too. The therapist has a subtle job to create an atmosphere in which the patient can speak and be listened to in a meaningful way without colluding with the anorexic's wish to avoid emotional contact.

Assessment is face to face, and often this is the preferred way of being in the sessions that follow for anorexics – even if they do avoid eye contact (Wilson, 1992). It has been thought that anorexics may feel too deprived and abandoned by being seen in a more conventional setup where they lie on the couch. I think that it depends on the patient. Anorexics may feel that they can only cope with a small amount of contact, and once a week is often all they can manage at first. My experience is that, after some time, once a week therapy becomes limiting for the therapist since the resistance to change of any kind in anorexia is substantial, and more sessions during the week are preferable. Nevertheless, the therapist may not be able to persuade an anorexic patient to attend more frequently and the weekly format has to be used.

Bulimic patients who are not reducing their weight pose different problems at assessment, especially if they fall within the borderline personality disorder category, which as we know, some 30 per cent do. One of the problems with all eating-disordered patients is that the transference can be very intense, as is the case for those with a borderline personality disorder. While the anorexic may not reveal what she feels, the bulimic is much more likely to express an 'early and powerful' transference (Farrell, 1995: 68). With Ellen I was in a position to see her over a period of time and to assess whether or not interpretations about what she said were helpful. In particular, I tried to pick up how she related to me. Although it turned out to be a fairly stormy therapy, Ellen was able to work in the transference. Ellen was seen in a student counselling service, which may have been a less authoritarian and threatening environment in her eyes than some other settings. The general attitude of students to a counselling service can be quite positive and in Ellen's case, linked in with her motivation to finish her degree. When someone with an eating disorder contemplates therapy they are contemplating giving up the solution (however pathological) to a set of internal problems. This makes it hard to engage patients. However, in a workplace setting or a student counselling centre the perceived benefits of therapy are perhaps concrete and tangible, there is obviously something to gain such as a qualification or career, as well as to lose. Such settings are also often less threatening to the individual's brittle sense of self-esteem.

Amy's assessment was also carried out over several sessions and a trial period of therapy commenced. This helped both parties obtain a realistic view of whether or not psychoanalytic therapy was of benefit. As this was a therapy carried out in private practice it was possible to set whatever arrangement seemed best. At the Tavistock Clinic, the young people that are seen are assessed over four sessions. It may well be that a fairly substantial amount of time for an assessment, especially one where the patient is encouraged to feel that they are also assessing what would be right for them, is the best approach. So many patients drop out after a first session if they do not feel they have an investment in the process. If eating-disordered people, women in particular, are very afraid of intrusion, then assessments will be especially prone to the erection of 'no-entry' barriers. It may be helpful to keep in mind the terrible loneliness that someone with an eating disorder may experience, and the fine balance between relieving that isolation and invading someone's private retreat.

## Management and liaison

One of the most problematic aspects of working with an eating-disordered person is the need for the clinician to feel that he or she can truly concentrate on the emotional issues underlying the disorder, and to be able to focus on the therapeutic relationship as the medium through which change is brought about. If an anorexic is unable to maintain weight, there may come a point at which a patient is at risk. Clinicians may manage this situation in different ways or there may be a policy in the institution, which the clinician must follow. What I have found helpful is to suggest that the anorexic not go below the weight she is at the time I meet her and when this has been very low I have asked the GP to monitor the weight until it stabilises. However, in the past I have worked quite closely with GPs who have known me and have trusted me as I have trusted them. When it comes to dealing with GPs one does not know, or with unfamiliar multidisciplinary teams, the therapist is in a perplexing situation. Often, unless there has been a working relationship or a history of a psychodynamic or psychoanalytic approach, liaison can be fraught. The issues of intrusion and privacy can get acted out in a disturbing way. Flanders (2001) described working with a severely disturbed young woman and facing up to the risk of incomprehension and mistrust in a multidisciplinary realm if she did not liase over her patient. She thought deeply about the issue and came to the conclusion that it was better for her to contain her own anxiety and the patient's anxiety by keeping her boundary as an analyst than risk getting embroiled in a situation with a set of professionals about whom she knew little and whose clinical approach was so different to her own. Some clinicians may find this far too detached and want to seek co-operation with other agencies. One cannot make assumptions about what might be offered by an agency. Where there is an opportunity to be in contact, the splitting possibilities and acting out possibilities need to be weighed up as well as the benefits. Another point of view is that one might seize on a possible contact with other professionals in order to deepen their understanding of the unconscious processes at work in the psychotherapy of eating disorders, and to help create a safe basis for liaison.

With Jenny, liaison with her GP was agreed to from the start as it was the GP who made the referral. I made explicit at assessment about what I thought would be the limits and responsibilities of the liaison. Similarly with Ellen, I had the benefit of liaison with a GP who was perceptive and supportive. At a time when I became very concerned about Ellen's steroid medication and its side-effects I decided to mention it to Ellen (she was becoming extremely aggressive in a way that just felt chemically induced to me). Ellen was able to go back to the clinic and get her medication checked and, indeed, there was a problem with it and the dosage was altered and the chemical quotient of her aggression vanished. Amy's GP was unknown to me and there was no direct contact. However, Amy was able to get advice from a dietician and medication from her GP to help her follow a healthier eating regime.

None of the patients mentioned needed admitting to hospital. People who are admitted may be offered a whole range of possible treatments, and be attended to by various professionals with diverse trainings and qualifications. Sometimes there is no one qualified or experienced to a very high level to help the patient. This is a difficult situation and again people will respond differently. It can sometimes be best to arrange to see the patient after their discharge from hospital, although others might argue that the continuation of the therapeutic relation throughout the in-patient stay is paramount.

If an anorexic is in hospital, perhaps being fed through a tube or according to a strict, enforced regime, it is certainly a time when a thoughtful person who can establish rapport may be the best means of support for the patient. Nurses on medical wards may have done some training and can adopt a counselling skills approach although often they are just too busy for this. Sometimes self-chosen starvation arouses great anger in those who come into contact with the patient or conversely a wish to protect and mother. Both of these responses are problematic. The patient can become seen as manipulative or more vulnerable than she is and be infantilised. It may be that some educational work would not go amiss with general hospital staff, but they cannot be expected to be skilled in every condition they come across. My feeling is that it is best to get patients back into the community as soon as one can, and attending therapy or counselling if they wish to make a commitment to it. Where there is no 'community' a psychiatric ward may be the only alternative. One of the reasons I wanted to approach this book from the premise that eating and its ramifications affect us all is that very thin or very obese people do have an impact on the emotional life of their helpers and may trigger off reactions that are linked to fears and anxieties within the helpers. Similarly people who vomit or purge can arouse extreme feelings in helpers, and sometimes it is cruelty that is whipped up. I saw a young bulimic woman as a crisis referral on a general ward in a local hospital. She had taken an overdose because she had become so depressed as well as bulimic, and had been sexually abused by a relative. As she came round on the ward, a nurse leaned over her and said 'we are angels and you are in heaven – you have died.' As the patient was so groggy it took her a while to realise that this was not true: she was alive and still in an abusive universe.

## Technique

Hopefully, some understanding of the approach I have found helpful in my own encounters with eating-disordered patients has come across in the previous chapters. Here, I would like to draw out some of the issues other commentators have raised about what works best with this patient group. For many years it was thought that a psychoanalytic approach to eating disorders, particularly anorexia, was to be avoided, mainly because of the extensive work carried out by Bruch. Perhaps, also because this was in a clinical climate where an analytic approach was more classic and quite different to the emphasis placed today on the patient's internal world and the subtle interplay of relationships with an internal and an external object, expressed within the analytic session, and commented upon by an analyst. Bruch found that her anorexic patients benefited most from an approach that was gently educational and which involved a certain amount of clarification and explanation. Farrell (1995: 66) suggested that a therapist may end up putting herself in an omniscient position by adopting such a role, and thereby feed into a phantasy of an all-powerful mother. Swift (1991) noted the importance of Bruch's findings but considers they are best understood as related to the therapeutic holding environment. He proposes that Bruch's seminal work should inform the therapist's attitude in the following way:

- Therapists should be led by what they find in their encounter with a patient, not by theory.
- Patients should be made collaborators in the therapeutic process.
- Therapists should avoid appearing cool and aloof but instead be warm and honest.
- The patient should be educated about what psychotherapy involves.
- The tone of sessions should not be over sombre.
- Patience is required.

However, Swift believed Bruch misunderstood the importance of transference interpretation and suggested that transference is inherent in the therapeutic situation and should be worked with, while recognising the need for the attunement represented above. He says: 'It is our duty to meld the best of the old and the new as we lay the groundwork for clinical and research efforts in the twenty-first century' (Swift, 1991: 65).

Barret and Fine (1990) found that direct interpretation was not helpful, but that gentle humour could sometimes reach patients. Wilson, commenting on both anorexia and bulimia which he sees as a psychosomatic disorder, suggested that even in very disturbed cases there is a split in the ego and some aspects of the ego function well enough to make use of the transference relationship (in Castelnuovo-Tedesco and Risen, 1988). Wilson argued for intensive analytic therapy for the young anorexic, and concurrent therapy for the parents with a colleague if necessary. He recommended face-to face-therapy in the first phase of treatment and suggested that medication should only be used as an adjunct when analytic therapy is not feasible. Both Wilson (ibid) and Schwartz (1986) found that in the early days interpretation of the patient's self-punishing and self-critical behaviour was tolerated by the patient. The therapist could go on subsequently to interpret the ways in which the patient defends against facing up to their masochistic behaviour. Only later, when the patient has a less critical superego, can interpretation be made of the destructive and the loving impulses and the conflicts they cause. Clearly the interpretation of Oedipal conflicts would come last in this scheme. Risen encouraged therapists not to give up too soon in trying to understand and comment upon the symbolic meaning of what the patient says (Castelnuovo-Tedesco and Risen, 1988).

Gehrie (1985) disputed the degree to which patients can cope with a rather sober, withholding ambience if a more 'classic' analytic approach is used and found his patients reacted by becoming intensely anxious and withdrawn and felt overwhelmed by isolation and incomprehension. He recommended, instead, that the therapist establish a relationship, which permits being used as an ideal 'archaic' object (this term is discussed below). The principle is to help create a structure in which symbolisation becomes possible.

Rizzuto found that in full analysis 'bulimarexic' patients did not develop a working alliance for a long time, even when they attended well and were committed to their treatment. In her view there is a fundamental problem of communication in these patients and she thought that: 'The analyst must carry out his/her lonely interpretive task, surviving insults and rejections. He/she must remember that behind the bravado of tough words and the indifference of shrugged shoulders hide a person and a child who suffer alone in a world without communication' (Rizzuto, 1988: 372). She tells us that the patient and the child within the patient long for an 'affectionate respect' which has been lacking, and the hostility suggested above has been a defence against giving in to the wish for closeness to an unresponsive or critical object who may reject them. Indeed, she says the defence against transference *is* the transference in such patients.

There are differences between patients, depending not only on symptomatology but also on age, character and underlying fundamental structural difficulties. How one works with a patient may also be affected by the setting in which one works. A lone practitioner in private practice may need to be more cautious than someone who can call upon other professionals to help deal with crises which are brought about as a response to the turbulence that analytic therapy causes.

Hamburg identified the function of bulimia in weaving together the patient's inner world and stressed the need to balance respect for the architect of the symptom with compassion for the sufferer so that there is a 'falling-together rather than falling apart' for the patient (Hamburg, 1989: 137) when the symptom is deconstructed in therapy. This is true for any patient, of course. However, pulling out a strand of meaning from the woof and warp of the patient's discourse without the patient unravelling is not always possible. It is the delicate nature of psychotherapy that too little a tug will be ineffective, and too strong a tug may cause a collapse. In full psychoanalysis it may be possible to contain a collapse and help the person knit themselves back together, but this might only be possible in psychotherapy and counselling where there is additional help from elsewhere, such as an inpatient facility or a team of professionals from several disciplines.

As mentioned already, eating disorders are a common pathway for a range of difficulties. Farrell thought that normal weight bulimics tended to be best able to make use of an interpretative approach while restricting anorexics were harder to reach this way. She thought the most difficult group were the anorexic bulimics because they were the most self-destructive of all the groups. Personally, I have found the length of time that someone has been expressing his or her difficulties through the medium of an eating disorder is also significant. When a person has a chronic problem, especially if it involves staying at a low weight for a long time, or indeed a high weight for a long time, therapy may be only partially successful. It is, however, unhelpful to generalise too much.

Some contemporary analytic practitioners are making efforts to combine elements of different therapeutic interventions. Reich and Cierpka detected an increase in this tendency, which has grown out of research or theoretical projects and clinical practice with bulimics (1998). Tobin and Johnson described at length ways in which behaviour therapy and psychodynamic therapy can be integrated in the treatment of eating disorders in general (1991). Johnson also recommended a more active involvement with borderline bulimics:

> The pathway to developing a healing therapeutic relationship with borderline bulimics is simultaneously simple and quite complicated. The primary task, from my perspective, is to demonstrate to the patients over the course of time that the therapist is committed, consistent, durable and reliable. Since I feel that the primary self-regulatory difficulty among the subgroup stems from neglect, the

therapist needs to err in the direction of being actively involved in the management of the patients' lives. (Johnson, 1991: 182)

Reich and Cierpka also stressed the opening phases of work with bulimics in particular, noting that they tend not to choose analytic therapy. This is not just because they do not want to give up the solution to the problem they have found in their eating disorder. They argued that it is because of a 'fear of confrontation with the inner self, particularly the parts of the self considered to be "defective", and the strong action orientation associated with it' (Reich and Cierpka, 1998: 394–5). They advocated paying special attention to diagnosis and proposed that the patient fill out an eating diary to help the therapist be more precise about what the patient does, but also to convince the patient that he or she is being taken seriously. This is meant to help the patient avoid feeling as if they are alone with their problems, and promotes a more active collaboration. After this opening phase of between 10 and 20 sessions the therapist can work in a more ordinary psychodynamic way. It is interesting how Bruch's ideas about education and clarification have found an expression in this concrete way. Practitioners vary in how they feel about persevering with their usual approach in the face of strong acting out tendencies. Reich and Cierpka proposed that their integrated model of treatment may be especially useful in the early stages of work with the most 'difficult' patients. While Reich and Cierpka may be right about the patients they come across, and there are probably many ways of developing therapeutic alliances, I want to stay within the psychoanalytic framework to consider what it might mean when patients encourage us to take a very different approach to our normal one. I do not wish to suggest that we do not moderate and adapt the way we work to our patients. After all, it is the basic rule of a psychoanalytic approach that the therapist follows the patient rather than forces their views on the patient, and we have been discussing once- and twice-a-week work, not psychoanalysis, but the way we adapt need not involve a change in the analytic attitude.

## Transference, countertransference and the analytic attitude

I would like to go right back to basics in reminding readers of one of the key papers on which the psychoanalytic notion of change is founded. Strachey (1934, 1969) examined very closely the kind of interpretation one could make to a patient, which would bring about change. He believed that change could only be brought about in small steps and that these steps consisted of the analytic therapist showing, by the kind of transference interpretations they made, that the way the patient was relating to them was on the basis of an earlier relationship which was construed in an unrealistic, infantile way. The therapist, by retaining a neutral stance, could make comments about such phenomena, which over time, produced in the mind of the patient an experience of a relationship of a new kind or a new object, as later on it became called (Baker, 1993). Such interpretations were considered mutative, that is, able to bring about lasting change. Similarly, where the therapist fails to maintain neutrality and, instead, repeats the earlier experience or tries to reassure the patient that he or she is not really that earlier figure, the opportunity for the patient to actually experience the difference is taken away. Reassurance becomes a way in which the analytic therapist encourages an archaic, idealised representation of a relationship – one that is as unrealistic as its opposite: an archaic bad object. The point of neutrality is that it permits a new relationship to be created on the basis of a more mature point of view. The analyst or therapist is not ideal or idealised, nor malevolent or denigrated but something new, different and good enough. In working with people with eating disorders this essential aspect of working from a psychoanalytic principle is challenged by the patient from the start.

Intending to make a transference interpretation goes against the grain: it requires the therapist to expose him or herself to a kind of danger since at the point at which the interpretation is made : 'the analyst is in fact deliberately evoking a quantity of the patient's id-energy while it is alive and actual and unambiguous and aimed directly at himself. Such a moment must above all others put to the test his relations with his own unconscious impulses' (Strachey, 1969: 292). Although this may sound like outdated terminology, the results of being related to as if one is ideal or awful, and the struggle to disentangle oneself from being at the receiving end of loving or hating impulses in order to say something about them, is familiar to us all. Of course, all patients put this principle to the test and some therapists and analysts would not agree that what is most mutative is such a transference interpretation.

## What is in the transfer to the therapist

The nature of working with people with eating disorders is such that keeping to a neutral and respectful stance, whereby one can even-handedly pay attention to all that the patient brings and to say something about it, is, to say the least, a strain. In this respect, it is not unlike working with people considered as having a borderline personality disorder, as mentioned earlier (Sohn, 1985). Sohn gave an account of how anorexic and bulimic patients share a common state of mind whereby either the desire for the object is denied, or the object's particular value is denied, and can be replaced by substitutions. The anorexic wishes to do away with appetite for any food and the bulimic lacks satisfaction with any food: always wanting more or different. As a consequence, the analyst or the therapist feels not valued, not wanted, not seen as even really existing in their own right, or not giving the right words, be they interpretations or not. Therapists can be lassooed into this unrewarding world and made to feel useless. In turn, feeling useless can nudge us into all sorts of behaviour. When I worked as part of a team on an in-patient ward for people with eating disorders and alcohol and drug problems it became quite a regular occurrence that a patient with either anorexia or bulimia would become the focus for a split in the nursing team over how to understand and treat the patient. It was usually the case that one group felt that the other group was being manipulated and was not maintaining an appropriate professional stance. Michael, who was mentioned in Chapter 4 became a 'special' patient in this way. The dynamics of the 'special' patient have been discussed elsewhere (Main, 1957). However, what interests me most here is the way in which the actual stance taken had been seen as at variance with the normal 'professional attitude' (Winnicott, 1960). In other words, there had been something happening in the countertransference that has either made for a deviation in practice or made one group fear it. It is this aspect of countertransference that I want to consider as a basis for understanding the complex and powerful responses that are common when working with people with eating disorders. That a team is divided shows what a powerful process is going on in a group of people. Within one individual the conflict is similar, and it becomes difficult to be dispassionate and much easier to take one side of a split in the countertransference.

If we think about the way the patient is trying to relate to us and the kind of object we seem to represent, it becomes clearer that the patient is returning to a certain kind of experience which, in principle, is one they have gone into therapy to avoid. This idea is well accepted by psychoanalytic practitioners, but the reality of constantly coming up against a challenge to therapeutic work, nonetheless, takes its toll on practitioners. There are several different ways of understanding the kind of internal state that is created and the kinds of object relations, which can be encountered. Sohn suggests that the therapist is made to experience the state of mind of the patient as both subject and object – the depriving and the deprived. Other analysts such as Sours and Sprince have found that there is a lack of differentiation or individuation at issue in the history of eating-disordered patients, particularly in women. Sometimes this can make the therapist feel as if she is kept outside of an emotional contact with the patient who seems untouchable or bland (Birksted-Breen discusses this in relation to anorexic patients, see 1989). The unreachability of such patients is difficult for us to bear: it is a wounding response to our professional and personal wish to be helpful and to succeed in our work. The anorexic patient prefers to use her own researches to produce interpretations about why she is as she is, and seems satisfied with them however superficial or hackneyed they may seem to us. We can get stirred up and want to push our therapeutic food at the anorexic patient in the face of this response to our work, or we may get very dispirited and bored. Both of these responses are a way of communicating important messages to us about the internal state of mind of the patient and how it is reproduced in ourselves from the perspective of the patient or of the patient's original object.

The bulimic patient takes in what we say then gets rid of it and we are left outside of this scene of throwing up what has been offered – the attempt to stop therapeutic food from getting into the system is kept secret and private. We are kept in a relation to the patient as useless and powerless, but nonetheless not quite fully gotten rid of either, if the patient continues to attend.

The patient who eats compulsively and becomes obese takes in what we have to give but it does not nourish or it only adds substance to a heavy state of mind. The obese patient devalues what we do – she can give herself plenty but it is taken in as something with which to hurt herself, not as nourishment. This helps her keep feelings and impulses at bay: she is anaesthetised.

## Hate in the countertransference

In thinking about the countertransference involved in working with people with eating disorders, I have found it useful to re-read the paper by Winnicott on hate in the countertransference. He encourages clinicians to accept hurtful, angry feelings towards the people they are trying to help, and to see these feelings not only as valid but as having meaning. We can use our own hate in the service of our work, but we need to think about it objectively and to distinguish hate that is justified in the circumstances (and we may want to do something with it at a later stage in the shape of an interpretation about it), and hate that is not. This pre-supposes that there is not a reservoir of hate in the therapist, belonging to past figures and situations and which has not been worked on by the therapist in a personal therapy or analysis. Winnicott felt that with neurotic patients the therapist takes on the role of a helpful figure from the patient's past: 'He cashes in on the success of those who did the dirty work when the patient was an infant' (1947: 197). In psychotherapy, perhaps it is most common to occupy the role of the good object or early parental figure rather than to seek the more analytic neutral role postulated by Strachey (Rosenfeld, 1972). Nevertheless, if this is the usual position, it is still one from which many patients try to get the therapist to deviate. Where a child has had no parents or parents who were not able to provide the necessary security, he or she may spend their time unconsciously seeking parents. They may not be able to believe in being loved until they have been hated. Winnicott thought one had to be able to understand one's own hate in order to think about another's rather than react to it at the time. A child needs hate in the environment to be able to hate, but he needs to be protected from knowing about it until he can cope with it. A therapist expresses hate by sticking to the end of sessions, giving himself holidays away from the patient, and only in very specific circumstances making it the basis of an interpretation (for example, involving the patient's debt to the therapist for what has been tolerated).

One of the common experiences of meeting with anorexic patients is that, at first, it is very difficult to detect any hate. Often an emaciated young woman will say how wonderful her parents are and the therapist will be struck by the surreal experience of seeing a teenager at her physical limits, thin, cold and either sad or euphoric, while hearing a sentimental story about the family. This may be a situation where the patient cannot hate satisfactorily and where sentimentality not love predominates. In the countertransference the therapist feels trapped: how can I tackle what is being denied, that is, the huge battle going on between the parents and the young woman? Why is the therapist being made to suffer? One answer might be therapeutic impotence. Another might be suppression of a normal alternative viewpoint. Whatever this particular scenario might communicate it does so not just at the level of the story the patient is telling, but the effect on the ability of the therapist to say what she thinks, or even think what she wants to think.

When a patient has had a very damaged early life, she or he may be more attached to the setting and the routines than to the therapist. Indeed Strachey, in his famous paper talked of the mutative interpretation as the key to change, but said it was like making a cake, and thought the currants (transference interpretations) were enormously important, but one could not make a cake from currants alone. Therapists need tact, empathy and a natural personal style suited to the work he or she undertakes, as well as the ability to make links and interpretations that are not related to the transference.

The idea of a 'no-entry' system of defences for anorexic patients who want to keep out the world (Williams, 1997) which has often involved a mother who has projected into the anorexic in childhood is useful. Williams has commented on the need to adapt her technique in that at first patients can only cope with 'small spoonfuls' of therapy, and that it is therefore a good idea for patients to start with a lower frequency of sessions. She may also employ a soft tone of voice and deliver her thoughts in a very careful way. This does not mean that she has become one-sided in her approach – she may be able to consider all the material the patient brings to her, but her response is at a level that the patient can manage. Neutrality does not mean standard or uniform – the therapist is giving a very particular kind of response to a very specific sort of situation. I wonder if some of the criticisms of a psychoanalytic approach in the past have come about in situations where the particular needs of the patient have not been followed. The contemporary approach encourages the clinician to think precisely about how their words are received by the patient and to follow and learn from what the patient does in response to them.

Williams also described work with patients who have been more 'porous' and where projections have got into them like 'foreign bodies'. Here the countertransference is different, there is a plea from the patient '... to tidy up ... to differentiate foreign bodies from what is nourishing and to internalise a filing system, an organising function of my own' (Williams, in Anderson and Dartington, 1998: 96).

Lawrence (2002) also noted the intrusiveness of the internal object in anorexia, in particular in female anorexics. She noted that nothing is taken in the normal way by either eating or intercourse, and that the mother is used to help the patient cover over her anxieties rather than is used by her to contain and overcome them. She believed the primitive tie to the mother has not been broken – that there is not a triangular space in the patient's mind in which she can symbolise. Something has gone wrong with her identification with the father. She described at some length the way this was experienced in the way her patient intruded into her – making her feel she was the intrusive one. The patient even had Lawrence convinced that the patient was sleeping with a neighbour of Lawrence's.

There are many competing perspectives on what has caused the state of affairs a therapist finds herself in when trying to work with a patient with an eating disorder, and to find the right quantity, quality and specificity of therapeutic food to give. The therapist is often extremely challenged in the countertransference and there seems little space in the patient to think about her experiences. I hope that this book has gone some way to helping others think about their experiences. However, a book is no substitute for good supervision and this will be discussed later.

## Body image

The research literature on anorexia nervosa abounds with references to distortion of body image, in particular, finding that some anorexics of low weight perceive their image in the mirror to be bigger than it really is (Bruch, 1962; Slade and Russell, 1973; Pierloot and Houben, 1978; Wingate and Christie, 1978; Garner and Garfinkel, 1981–82; Kalliopuska, 1982; Horne et al., 1991).

Unfortunately, establishing the quality and extent of body-image distortion is confused by a lack of consistency over methods of measurement employed, age groups studied, duration of anorexia and disagreement about what exactly is being measured (Warah, 1989) and whether or not restricting-type and binge-eating/purging-type anorexics are both included (Garner and Garfinkel, 1981–82).There are other problems too: Halmi (1977) for example, found that normal female adolescents tended to overestimate their body-size. Crisp and Kalucy (1974); Button et al. (1977); Buree et al. (1984) and Whitehouse et al. (1988), all found no evidence to support the argument that anorexics are particularly prone to perceptual distortions. Probst et al. (1992) found that anorexics and non-anorexics alike underestimated body-size, whereas Penner et al. (1991) found anorexics and non-anorectic thin people, both overestimated body-size. Studies have not been carried out in a systematic way with similar patient groups so the results are not conclusive.

What is striking from the literature is the range of bizarre sounding techniques used:

- The Caliper Device (Slade and Russell, 1973).
- The Image Marking Procedure (Askevold, 1975).

- The Distorting Photograph Technique (Garner *et al.*, 1976).
- Three Different Video Monitor Procedures (Allebeck, 1976; Meerman, 1983; Pierloot and Houben, 1978; Wingate and Christie, 1978; Freeman *et al.*, 1984; Touyz *et al.*, 1984; Probst *et al.*, 1992).
- The Distorting Mirror Technique (Brodie *et al.*, 1988, 1994).

Participants in experiments may also act compliantly to please the researchers (Norris, 1984) throwing further doubt on the findings. Furthermore, what is being measured is a perceptual distortion as represented visually, for example, by using photographs and drawings, without any analysis of that representational system. Like Fisher (1973) I query the validity of measuring perceptual distortion in relation to geometric illusions: it is as if one distortion can be measured by another distortion.

There are many problems in assessing the veracity of body-size perceptual distortion. Indeed, disturbance in the way the body's weight or shape is experienced, rather than perceived, is now a diagnostic criterion for anorexia nervosa in *DSM IV* and *ICD-10*. Prior to 1994, *DSM III* and *DSM III-R* included distortion of perception of body image as a diagnostic criterion: the change in wording reflects the difficulties encountered in researching the concept. Establishing the existence of experiential disturbance, which is greater than the 'norm' is also problematic. The issue seems difficult to resolve.

More importantly for us, the unconscious meaning of the anorexic's statements or behaviours require exploration: for many years it was thought that anorexics did not feel hunger simply because they denied they did. The empirical experiments listed do not explain the meaning of the anorexic experience of looking and being seen in the mirror. There is even less evidence of a distortion in the perception of men with eating disorders, or bulimics of either sex. Obese people have trouble rightly estimating their size, but so do many people. The relationship to a true belief and the evaluation of size in an objective way is unclear. Some have suggested that it is something of a myth that anorexics have a distorted body image or have doubts about the way researchers understand it so concretely (Farrell, 2003).

Male body image and its relationship to an eating disorder is different to what one would anticipate. Men without an eating disorder are split as a group: half think that they should be bigger and half think that they should be smaller. Men who body build in gyms have been researched and interestingly have been found to have a history of anorexia in greater proportion than the average population of men

(Pope, Katz and Hudson, 1993). A group of men seem to be emerging as a research population who feel they are much smaller than they actually are and work on increasing their bodies in a compulsive way, much like anorexics do to lose weight and have been described by the researchers just mentioned as 'reverse anorexics'. What these different findings mean is obscure. However, they do all seem to support the idea that working on the body as a solution to one's troubles, or attempts at self-improvement is a ubiquitous strategy for dealing with underlying distress. The unconscious meanings attached to an apparent perceptual distortion are much more the stuff of psychotherapeutic intervention and need to be approached with great sensitivity, connecting as they do with core issues of sexual and gender identity.

## Men with eating disorders: gender identity and body image

Gender is a significant factor in the development of eating disorders, but for men, it seems sexuality is also. The research about men is much less substantial. Approximately 20 per cent of men with eating disorders identify as homosexual, double the estimated proportion of homosexual men in the population (Andersen and Bowers, 1999). The reasons for these divergences in gender and sexuality are not clear. There is less cultural endorsement for thinness and slimming amongst men, although this is changing, and the 'body beautiful' is more of an issue for some gay men. A specific trigger in men is childhood bullying about being overweight. Body builders and men who exercise a lot may have a form of eating disorder, which is not recognised as such. Specific occupations including athletics and jockeying seem to be linked to a higher incidence of eating disorders in men. Whereas some women may be concerned with body weight, men may be more bothered about body shape and muscles (Lloyd, 1997). 'Whilst men who became anorexic after feeling they were fat actually were 15 per cent over ideal bodyweight, women thought that they were fat at 90 per cent of ideal bodyweight. So men actually were overweight when they thought they were' (Copperman, 2000). Therefore, it appears that women thought they were 'fat' when they were not and men thought they were 'fat' when they were slightly above an 'ideal' weight for men.

Conflict over gender identity or over sexual orientation may be linked with the development of eating disorders in males. The evidence we have about men is confusing, especially as eating disorders seem to be a pathway for so many different issues, and body image may be connected more to unconscious processes than easily assessed conscious ones. Psychoanalytic work with men with eating disorders presents a much more convincing explanation about why gender identity and an eating disorder can be interrelated. Schneider (1991) reviewed seven of his clinical cases and discussed the way in which a boy's relationship to his core gender identity may be affected in a similar way to how his relationship with food is affected. Schneider did not differentiate between anorexics and bulimics, as the same fundamental dynamics, he believes, are at work in both syndromes. He considered the way in which both boy and girl children have their prime object relationship with their mother in early life. The girl can identify with mother and grow up identified as a woman, but the boy must disidentify with mother and also identify with father if he is to grow up to be identified as a man. For this to happen there needs to be someone who can take the role of being a father, though mother must play her part in letting go of her son and of being able to esteem the role of the father. Some analysts believe only an 'other' figure is needed, not necessarily a father and some like Green (Kohon, 1999) think there needs to be in mother's mind an idea of a third term, not necessarily a father. American, British and French schools of psychoanalysis diverge on the extent the father must be a real or a phantasy object. The role of the 'other' or 'father' is essential in the development of the capacity to symbolise as we have already seen. Without this capacity, there is a tendency for loss to be dealt with by concrete replacements: food for love, for example.

Disturbance in the relationship with the father or the mother's relationship with the father may make it hard for a boy to both disidentify with mother and identify with father. He may develop a tendency to make symbolic equations with food, and furthermore, his gender may not become differentiated so as to allow him to separate properly from his mother. The confusion over gender may also affect what it means for the boy to take either a man or a woman as his love object. Schneider found that men who identified as homosexual in a highly masculine way tended not to have eating disorders. He thought that what was most at stake in bulimia, in particular, was a gender identity problem, not a homosexual choice of love object. He suggested: 'In bulimic men, there is an effort to repair the disturbance in masculinity through incorporative and expulsive means. Bulimic men behave as though they believe that relatedness is established by eating and separateness by purging' (1991: 204–5). The kind of fathers that Schneider heard about were violent, abusive or disgusting in some way, or made to appear so by a pathological mother.

The boy who kept running, 'Michael', had been in violent abusive situations with several of his mother's partners, and seemed to not wish to develop a more powerful body or to be identified as a grown-up man. He found the relationship between myself and my female co-leader in the group difficult to tolerate. I think I was the father in his mind, although only briefly as he could not bear to stay with us in the group. It may be that other factors were at play – for example some of the men who were consulted in the review carried out for the Eating Disorders Association were unhappy at being the only man in a group. Several asked for more services for men and to meet other men with eating disorders. They also felt many of the issues that concerned them, concerned women too, and they did not want particularly to have male professionals helping them. Michael, as you will remember, was a patient who could divide a team of staff over his treatment plan. Perhaps as well as splitting off his feelings and projecting some of them into one group while having a more idealised relationship with the other, he also stopped them functioning creatively together as a team.

## Supervision

Psychotherapists and counsellors are used to having regular consultative meetings with senior colleagues where they discuss their clinical work. This kind of supervision is essential, especially as the countertransference impact of people with eating disorders is considerable. Other professions do not necessarily regularly have such support, but may benefit enormously from the opportunity to discuss their work with someone who can understand the stresses and strains of multidisciplinary working with people with eating disorders. Often, in specialist organisations, the most experienced and qualified person may be used to best effect in doing a good deal of supervision. As mentioned earlier the unconscious splitting and divisive processes that can be mobilised by patients are formidable. Furthermore, there will always be some members of staff who are uncomfortable with their own relationship to food and to their body and their anxieties can also easily be mobilised. In specialist agencies there may well be a number of very difficult patients, some with borderline personality disorder, and the emotional turbulence that they create can be overwhelming. The fear of losing patients who are starving to death or acting out in dangerous ways can create burnout in dedicated professionals. Supervision helps but workers also need a balance of cases in their workload, and opportunities to develop their understanding through continuing professional development.

An eating disorder is a symptom, and what may lie underneath may be extremely challenging to a person's ability to contain projections or to their capacity to use their sensitivity creatively. I cannot help but think that psychotherapists and counsellors need a mix of patients and levels of disturbance in order to hone their skills and to prevent them from becoming therapeutically one-sided in their thinking about eating disorders. They need to be open to new ideas about psychotherapy in general. There may be some drawbacks to working in specialist eating disorder services for staff, but on the other hand, specialised groups can be run, expertise can be built up, services aimed at men can be pioneered and research and evaluation can be carried out more effectively. Finally, supervision can only go so far in helping people – a good personal therapy and a good training are indispensable if people want to go further than their skills and background have so far enabled them.

---

Some key points

- The opening phase of psychotherapy is especially critical in the therapy of eating disorders.
- Assessment is best carried out over a period of time and the assessor may be the best person to see the patient for psychotherapy.
- A light touch is important at assessment and the patient should be encouraged to feel it is a collaborative project.
- The relationship with external agencies such as GP or mental health team members may be necessary but may also undermine the therapeutic relationship if it is not carefully managed on both sides (i.e. therapist and agency).
- Great sensitivity is required about the nature, timing and level of interpretations and the language and tone in which they are delivered.
- The psychotherapist should expect a struggle to be able to find a standpoint from which to consider the material in an even-handed 'neutral' way.
- Countertransference will be a vital clue to processes going on in the patient and between the therapist and the patient.
- Body image distortion may reflect underlying anxieties about the self and its relation to objects, in a complex way.
- Some male patients may have particular difficulties with their core gender identity.
- Supervision is helpful whether the work carried out is psychotherapy, counselling or a less formal approach.

---

# 7

# CONCLUDING THOUGHTS

The particular stresses and strains in the countertransference when working with people with eating disorders were discussed in Chapter 6. The best way in which a therapist can clarify and learn from what he or she discovers in working with people with eating disorders is first of all to undertake a training in psychotherapy alongside a personal therapy for themselves, if they have not already done so. Second, they should find a source of good psychoanalytic supervision. Short courses can also be of tremendous help in developing skills and understanding, and most importantly to share experiences and to learn from them, however experienced the practitioner may be. Attending conferences and clinical meetings are also useful, as is reading and keeping up with current clinical thinking in journals and books.

Each patient needs to be met in psychotherapy with an open mind and assumptions should not made about them. However, in listening to patients and trying to find out how they have got into their present states, it can be helpful to feel equipped with some usable concepts. Some helpful theoretical constructs, used in understanding processes that occur in psychotherapy and in the inner world, and to which I have referred throughout the book are summarised below:

- Psychic retreats
- Psychotic parts of the mind
- Symbolic equation
- Negation
- Mental space

These will be discussed in turn before I go on to consider eating disorders in relation to psychosomatic disorders, self-harm and sexual abuse. Subsequently, I revisit the cultural context of eating disorders, and touch upon the more people-related context of families and friends of those with an eating disorder before finally ending with some thoughts about research.

## Psychic retreats

John Steiner developed the notion of a psychic retreat in his clinical work with patients who not only withdrew emotionally in their analysis and who were then hard to make contact with, but who retreated frequently in this way or who were inaccessible for long periods of time. Temporary, fleeting withdrawal is easily understood – people need to be able to pull back if they feel too threatened by the emotional contact a therapist may make with them. However, some people, particularly borderline or psychotic patients, can ensconce themselves in a psychic retreat which impedes development. Sometimes a retreat is a reaction to an intrusive or hurtful comment from the therapist but with some patients even a very thoughtful and sensitive approach can trigger off a withdrawal. Steiner believed that such withdrawals are linked to a system of defences operating in the individual, which he has called 'pathological organisations of the personality'. These are systems of psychic defence which help the individual avoid anxiety by avoiding contact with other people and reality. Such a withdrawal may have a pictorial corollary, and may be experienced as a particular place such as an island or a building. Alternatively, it may be represented as a kind of organisation or gang. In Chapters 4 and 5 the main clinical examples both involve descriptions of a psychic retreat: in the case of Ellen it is an old building, in the case of Amy a fantasy place conjured up by eating chocolate and drinking fizzy drinks. The tyrannical nature of such organised defences is often easy to spot but they can also be idealised, and it is the therapist, not the patient then who feels restricted and blocked by the organisation. Such places of safety are retreated to as necessary, and the therapist has to begin to understand the process and to say something about the withdrawal at a time when they feel it can be heard. Sometimes the withdrawal is prolonged and the clinical work seems to be stuck in the doldrums. The patient has found a self-sufficient way of surviving without having to face painful reality, and if provoked by the threat of change may withdraw deeper. Readers will, I am sure, recognise this state of affairs as the mental state of many patients with chronic eating disorders, when misery prevails in the retreat but it is experienced as preferable to the devastation of change or emotional contact with the self and others.

Steiner believed that the defensive organisation described is a result of the destructiveness of the individual which, for a variety of reasons, has not been moderated in a more successful way. The role of external reality is unclear in the development of such defences, and many analysts have written about something similar linked to internal primitive feelings. Steiner tells us: 'Traumatic experiences with violence or neglect in the environment leads to the internalisation of violent disturbed objects which at the same time serve as suitable receptacles for the projection of the individual's own destructiveness' (Steiner, 1993: 4).

An important aspect of a pathological organisation is the way in which projective identification is used to split off unacceptable feelings and to locate them elsewhere. Aggression, for example, may be located in others and, if the individual cannot reverse the projective process, as most of us can do some of the time, it leaves him or her with a personality depleted of a link to his or her own aggression. Others then have a surplus of aggression attributed to them and the self is deprived of the full use of its own aggression. The idea of an anorexic looking critically at herself in the mirror comes to mind. The look she projects there is merciless. The way she imagines other people looking at her is hostile. Meanwhile she is unassertive about everything except not eating.

Clearly, it is hard work to keep on seeing a patient who has retreated and tempting for a clinician to retreat likewise. Sometimes the patient gets a perverse satisfaction from the retreat and becomes addicted to it, so that it is not just a place of safety and defence but it is also gratifying.

## Psychotic parts of the mind

Steiner's depiction of a psychic retreat owes something to Bion's paper on the non-psychotic and psychotic parts of the mind, as Steiner himself tells us. Bion, having analysed patients who were schizophrenic, came to the conclusion that even in the mind of the schizophrenic there were areas of functioning which were not psychotic, and similarly that in the 'severe' neurotic patient one finds areas that are psychotic. Bion applied Freud's work on the neuroses and psychoses to his own experiences with very ill patients. Freud distinguished neurotics in the way that their ego will split off unwanted parts of the id in the service of adapting better to reality whereas the psychotic will, in the service of the id, withdraw the ego from part of reality (Freud, 1924). Bion found in his most psychotic patients that the ego was never totally withdrawn from reality. Instead, contact with reality is dominated by an omnipotent phantasy, which is intended to wipe out reality or awareness of it. The part of the ego that is in contact with reality is subject to neuroses though it will be masked by the psychotic part. Here thus exist two parallel functioning parts of the personality. In psychotherapy this often means that while one part of the patient can respond to interpretations and other interventions, there may be another part which is much more disturbed and withdrawn. In eating disorders there is a wide spectrum of difficulties as has been mentioned numerous times, and even within some of the less apparently severe cases there may be psychotic processes at work. However, these terms do not imply that the person is psychiatrically psychotic. There is a difference between how psychoanalytic therapists use the idea of psychotic functioning and how psychiatrists do. In psychotherapy, unless one is working specifically with patients diagnosed as having major psychiatric disorders of a psychotic kind, it denotes more a primitive, irrational way of relating to the world where people may be seen by the patient more as part objects than whole real autonomous others. Where there is a lot of splitting and projective identification going on, 'psychotic' is often linked by therapists to the word 'process', to indicate that similar forces are at work as in schizophrenia but that the outcome may not be the same. Bion was, in fact, working as a psychiatrist, and his ideas devolve from that practice as well as psychoanalysis. However, non-medical psychotherapists use the same term too. Even so, some people with eating disorders may be masking an underlying psychotic disorder or borderline state in the psychiatric sense too.

In the psychotic part of the personality, the splitting that has been mentioned fragments the ego and projects bits of it into objects. As Bion puts it: 'The sadistic attacks on the ego and on the matrix of thought, together with projective identification of the fragments, make it certain that from this point on there is an ever-widening divergence between the psychotic and non-psychotic parts of the personality until at last the gulf between them is felt to be unbridgeable' (Bion, 1967: 51). While the neurotic will feel in conflict over feelings and ideas and will be able to sustain the introjection back into the ego of split off affects, the psychotic may find it unbearable. The psychotic person may retreat even deeper when facing loss and may attack his or her own mind in order not to be aware of loss. The non-psychotic will be able to think, symbolise and mourn.

## Symbolic equations

The capacity to think, to use symbols and to face loss are interrelated. Hanna Segal, developed an understanding of symbol formation derived from Klein's work on the two main defence systems we create in infancy: the paranoid-schizoid position and the depressive position. The paranoid-schizoid position is a stage where people are related to as part objects, and is succeeded by a stage where people are related to as whole objects – the depressive position. In the paranoid-schizoid position good and bad are kept apart as experiences and the object is seen as either a wholly good object or a wholly bad one. Where the good part-object is lost, a concrete bad one is felt to be in its place. Loss is never fully experienced – a persecuting bad object slips into its place. This process evolves so that eventually when a good part-object is lost, a substitute can be found and related to, but this would be not as a true symbol but as a concrete alternative. When we are more mature and recognise other people as being separate and combining good and bad aspects in the same person, we can feel devastated when they leave us. Hopefully for most of us this is a short-lived experience and we learn to fill the gap in the wait for them to return with a mental picture of them, and later maybe a word or thoughts about them. The *Fort-Da* game that Freud described (1920) is a good example of the process of coming to terms with a lost object which stands in for mother in the first instance, and acquiring the capacity for language in the bargain. He described the way a baby at a certain stage will repeatedly throw a toy out of the pram and someone will usually bring it back to the baby's great pleasure. After a while, the word 'gone/*fort*' may be added by the baby and another one like 'there/*da*' when it is returned. Symbols or words have replaced the substitute itself. The loss is replaced by a sense of mastery (although this is illusory). Nonetheless, the baby's development is facilitated. If the individual has not progressed to the stage where losses have been anodyne enough to permit their accommodation within psychic strategies that belong to a maturing mind, they have to be dealt with some other way. What may happen is that only a concrete substitute can be tolerated, and is related to as the real thing that is lost. Instead of being like a true symbol that has characteristics belonging to the symbol which are not the same as the original object, it is seen as just the same and conflicts and feelings related to the original object are drawn into the relation to it. Through projective identification part of the ego is identified with this special kind of entity via a process which Segal (1957) named a 'symbolic equation'. Only by being able to give up external objects and mourn their loss can the individual gain the capacity to be truly creative and make use of symbols as symbols.

## Negation

Negation is commonly found as a defence in eating disorders. It is worth reminding ourselves about this concept which is so intimately tied up with action instead of thinking. Freud discussed the way in which the unconscious mind has no concept of 'no' (Freud, 1925). The ego, however, may recognise something unacceptable in the unconscious, such as for example, one's own wish to be hurtful, by saying out loud that 'no! one does not have this wish!' We have all been accosted by acquaintances who say 'I'm not being rude but have you put on some weight?' thus offending without guilt. Negation involves partly recognising what has been repressed by way of an intellectual disclaimer while the bulk of the wish or impulse continues to be active but repressed in the unconscious. Negation permits one to deny a loss while continuing to have a repetitive, compulsive relationship with its substitute, food, making it a powerful factor in maintaining eating disorders.

## Mental space

Mental space was discussed briefly in relation to the work of Donald Meltzer in Chapter 3 and applied to understanding how little mental space the anorexic seemed to have available to her for experiencing emotion. Creating a space in which a psychotherapy can take place is one of the central concerns of this book. There is much more that has been thought about in relation to mental space by other writers (see Young, 1994 for a wide-ranging discussion of the history of the concept and its applications outside of clinical practice). However, the aspect I wish to illuminate further is that for a fully functioning creative mind to come into being, the individual needs to have been able to internalise both a good experience of a mother figure and a of another person who is different to mother – this may be a father but sometimes it is not. Birksted-Breen (1996) found that some of her patients who seemed to be trying to identify themselves as beyond needs and vulnerability, or even beyond the human condition, suffered from a wish for fusion and a terror of being annihilated when their wish for fusion was indulged in any way. They were in a kind of seesaw trap where separateness was feared and being linked to another was feared. The capacity to internally link thoughts and feelings together and to consider at leisure without a pull to act or get rid of an experience was reduced in such people. They could not take a perspective on themselves. The link between self and other was similarly problematic. Birksted-Breen thought that the internal space in which the processing of emotion and experience could take place needed to come about by the satisfactory resolution of the Oedipus complex in one particular way. She argued that unless the link between mother and father could be internalised, the linking function within was jeopardised. The individual turned to a more omnipotent mode of being where he or she had to be self-sufficient and without needs like an all-powerful phallus. This phallic way of being which is associated with black and white thinking is very common in eating-disordered people. The alternative, the internalisation of the link between the parents, the 'penis-as-link' function of the father (or someone occupying that position in relation to the individual's primary object), structures internal space. The penis-as-link honours the bisexuality of the mind and establishes a kind of triangular interiority where there is a self, an other and an other's other. Needs do not feel such a threat and closeness does not extinguish the individual.

Lawrence (2002) commented on the presence of an intrusive internal object in anorexia and links this finding with thoughts about the meaning of the preponderance of female sufferers. She saw the lack of an internal space in which symbolisation can take place as a result of a symbiosis with mother, with the girl using the mother as a shield to overcome anxieties rather than to help her work through them. In such cases the primitive tie to the mother has not been broken by internalising father's function as 'penis-as-link' (Birksted-Breen, 1996), or to put it in another way, his structuring effect on the child's mind as the 'other' who has a previous, more intimate, claim on mother.

Schneider (1991) identified a related pattern in men with eating disorders who may suffer from a core gender anxiety and whose eating disorder is a solution to being unable to resolve a difficulty of identification which appears to be linked to an absence of a positive father figure, linked in a constructive way with the mother. One might hypothesise that they have been unable to internalise a 'penis-as-link' too. The importance of this aspect of the Oedipus complex for femininity and masculinity is underlined, and its vicissitudes implicated in eating disorders. Furthermore, Lawrence's discussion of anxieties about intrusion in anorexia applies equally to the bulimic patient and the obese patient featured in the main clinical illustrations in the book. There seems to be a unifying theme in at least these cases – where there is a failure of penis-as-link the patient may experience attempts by the therapist or analyst at linking as the sense of an intruding object.

## Psychosomatic disorders

It is quite unusual, in my experience, to find only one symptomatic 'condition' in any person who seeks psychotherapy, and when anyone becomes depressed there are usually reverberations in home and work life, as well as in sleep and eating patterns. It is also extremely common to find that a disorder of eating occurs or has occurred in the past. Many people who do not see themselves as having an eating disorder may seek help for other reasons. Psychosomatic disorders are very common and may co-exist with an eating disorder as they do with so many other states of mind which require help. The links between the mind and the body are mysteriously interwoven so that the capacity to elaborate a psychological conflict in one area of functioning does not seem to preclude a tendency to somatise in another area. Indeed, sometimes the category of eating disorder, in particular, anorexia, is lumped together with other, more evident psychosomatic entities such as asthma and irritable bowel syndrome, as if it were a psychosomatic disorder (see Kaufman and Heiman, 1964; Zerbe, 1993). Others (Temple, 2003) disagree with such a way of understanding anorexia. Some clinicians also distinguish between the notion of a psychosomatic illness, which after all has a known physical base, if not a known cure, and the broader, less traditionally illness-linked idea of somatisation. One of the benefits of working longer term with patients, and especially if it is possible to see them at a more intense frequency, is that the clinician comes to see the shifts between the mind and the body as a site for unhappiness, maybe even pain, across a period of time and sometimes within one session. Sometimes the shift is much more like Freud's 'mysterious leap from mind to body' leaving the clinician in a helpless state with a patient who is hard to reach and cannot be soothed. Exactly how to place eating disorders in relation to categories like psychosomatic illness, hysteria and alexithymeia is a conundrum which merits far more analysis and intellectual endeavour than this book is able to provide. Self-harm is yet another classification within which eating disorders have sometimes been considered. There are also other categories, which have been proffered as sources of understanding about possible causes of eating disorders such as childhood sexual abuse.

If we take psychoanalytic explanations about what might be happening at an unconscious level, in the inner life of someone with an eating disorder, it becomes easier to understand why sometimes the struggle that is perceived around food and the body gives way to a similar struggle around a different set of relations or activities. The important issue for practitioners is that a solution to an inner dynamic is sought, and its particular characteristic is affected by psychotherapy, by developmental changes, by the world at large, and by the particular psyche-soma configuration of the individual. However, we do need to know when such developments are part of a resurgence of symptoms linked to ending, a resistance, a deterioration or the plain working through of psychotherapeutic material. It takes time to know this and it is not possible to generalise, but it may be useful to consider some specific issues.

## Irritable bowel syndrome (IBS)

One condition which seems to be commonly suffered by bulimics, in particular, is irritable bowel syndrome. This has sometimes been seen as 'an angry gut' (Read, 2000) in patients for whom expression of negative emotions like anger and hate is inhibited. Instead, the individual seems to turn an angry attack upon themselves and suffers as a consequence. This is very much along the lines of a moral defence as argued by Fairbairn (1952) whereby the outside world and people in it are preserved from attack by an internal closed circuit. This may be the origin of a tendency to hold bad feeling states inside, although it may also be that the individual concerned is especially vulnerable to pain and inflammation in this area and conflicts then irritate this site, as McDougall has suggested (1989). Other negative feelings such as jealousy and envy may also be dealt with in this way: it is as if the gut doesn't exactly help the emotional processing of difficult feelings but takes them on in a concrete way and really cannot then cope with this bad food. Of course, bulimics can suffer a range of health problems as a consequence of their binge–vomit/purge regimen, but such physical consequences are usually distinct from a psychosomatic illness. However, it is possible that IBS can be precipitated by bulimia. The relationship between irritable bowel symptoms and emotional upset is described next in a clinical vignette.

John was a man in his twenties who had never fully resolved his feelings about an emotionally fragile and disturbed mother, who suffered from periodic bouts of mental illness. At times she was clearly a loving mother and he identified with her go-getting career aspirations when she was well and he, too, strived to excel as a designer, like her. However, he found the experience of anger and open expression of hate unthinkable when he began psychotherapy for a constellation of difficulties including disordered eating and, at a secondary level, IBS. Inevitably, in the course of therapy, he had to face the anxiety and disappointment of separations from his therapist during holiday breaks. This made him furious and, after some time, he was able to express his anger and disbelief that his therapist could leave him just (to his mind) like his mother had done when she was ill. The step forward in being able to express his emotions directly was followed usually by a resurgence of his IBS and a concomitant sense of persecution: his therapist must be incompetent or cruel to expect him to cope with being left. Eventually, the physical pain would subside to some extent, and an insight would start to develop about his separation anxiety and its links to his IBS and to his eating, but would then dissolve under the pressure from his hatred of the fact that no perfect mother–infant couple could be resurrected. As his therapy progressed this pattern was worked on again and again: here the IBS might be considered as part and parcel of a particular set of relations the patient needed to work on in relation to his internal state and to the therapist in the transference. However, the challenge to a therapist who offers psychotherapy as an alternative medium to a well-established, internal closed circuit should not be underestimated. This, of course is true for any clinical set-up where a long established coping strategy must be traded in for a way of relating to the self and others that is far more complex.

## Self-harm

Eating disorders are sometimes seen as belonging to a range of self-harming activities such as cutting and parasuicide. Gardner (2001) includes eating disorders in her very helpful book on self-harm which draws on her extensive experience as a psychotherapist working with this client group. However, in relation to a particular agency in which she worked she noticed: '... out of the fifteen young women with symptoms that included cutting, hitting and burning themselves, eight had stopped those symptoms by the time psychotherapy had ended, while with one it was not really clear. Three were unfortunately left with their long-established eating disorder, although the other forms of self-harm had stopped' (Gardner, 2001: 7). She seemed to imply that eating disorder is a fundamentally more difficult arena in which to bring about change. It is difficult to see which is paramount: the clinician's expertise in one area and, perhaps, less familiarity with another, or the intransigence of disordered eating. I have always been struck about how often thoughts or fantasies about self-harm come up in psychotherapy with women and agree with her that disordered eating and self-harm often co-exist. Gardner, perhaps echoing Anderson (1998), uses the idea of an 'adolescent state of mind' to unify some of the themes she has discovered such as the tendency to action rather than thought and the use of the body as a forum for self-destruction. She links this to what she calls ' the encaptive conflict'. Gardner posits a captivation by an avaricious, overwhelming mother from whom the individual cannot separate and about whom she feels ambivalence (Gardner, 2001: 143). The emphasis on adolescent acting out rather than thinking is especially helpful in understanding the patient, whatever the age of the patient.

Ellen (see Chapter 4) only revealed in the last few weeks of her therapy that she had been cutting her legs before and during her five year therapy. I constantly felt lacerated in the sessions with her – she seemed to hate me with a passion that bordered on insane at times. Although her cutting seemed to have stopped, it was the last bastion of her desire to maintain a private, perverse area in which she could indulge a ritualised and pathological self-soothing, which also satisfied a cruel instinct that destroyed the good holding me identified with her skin. Self-cutting emerged in the discourse of the session (as far as I know) and was not returned to in practice: Ellen put into words a last part of the secret her she had been nursing for so long rather than acting it out. Here the self-harm appeared as part of the work of ending. It is interesting though to cast my mind back to a key image of Ellen's therapy. Early on she had described, vividly, a childhood habit of hiding in a dangerous yet paradoxically, safe place where she would suffer scratches from the barbed wire she had to climb through but would be inaccessible to anyone else and at peace with herself. This image spoke volumes about her but did not, at the time, alert me to what she did, literally, in between sessions to regain her self-reliance and to keep me out.

Regarding parasuicide, I have found this to be much less common in people I have worked with who have eating disorders. I think the eating disorder saves them from parasuicide, normally. If the person wants to kill themselves, they will try to do so and will probably succeed, but once engaged in therapy, my own experience is that this is no greater a problem than with any other kind of patient or client.

## Sexual abuse

Sexual abuse in childhood is often mentioned in connection with eating disorders, but it is a complicated connection. Lask and Bryant-Waugh (2000) saw no evidence for the claim that there is a strong connection although many people who have been sexually abused go on to suffer a range of mental health problems. Most people who develop an eating disorder have not been sexually abused according to the review carried out by Lask and Bryant-Waugh. However, Wooley (1991) commented that many of the women who attend her residential unit for the treatment of bulimia had suffered some kind of sexual abuse: 59 per cent were victims of incest, rape or childhood molestation (Kearney-Cooke, 1988). Levy and Adams (1998) argued a more subtle point which is that unwanted sexual experience may encourage obsessionality, which itself predisposes to developing an eating disorder. Yet Reich and Cierpka (1998) found sexual abuse is no more common in people with eating disorders than it is in any other form of severe mental illness, though it can be a considerable factor all the same. The issue is reviewed in a paper by Connors and Morse (1993). MacSween surveyed a group of 35 anorexic women and enquired about their feelings in relation to sexuality. This slant was partly prompted by Caroline O'Toole of Glasgow Anorexic Aid who suggested that most anorexics feared or disliked sexual contact, and often did not like to be touched at all. MacSween found that 30 out of 35 feared or disliked sex and a number of them volunteered that they felt uncomfortable being touched or having their personal space encroached upon. One respondent said: 'I cannot cope with anyone coming close or touching me on the shoulders or back, the emotional pain hurts, I cringe so much I want to curl into a ball and hide, I feel like barbed wire' (MacSween, 1993: 221–2).

What is common is a lack of consideration about personal boundaries of any kind, sexual or emotional, especially in bulimia. Some highly disturbed individuals who have developed eating disorders have been sexually abused as children but they have often been traumatised in other ways too. These are people who have not only had to struggle with deprivation, trauma and conflicts but who have almost constructed a way of being around a self that is constantly and severely punished in a variety of ways. I have written briefly elsewhere (1999) about Cora, a woman who had been fasting, exercising and purging for many years when I met her. Cora had been sexually abused by her father, in the presence of her mother who ignored her plight. She had become a disruptive and disturbed child, presumably trying to express something about her predicament by stealing and vandalism, and was put into care and deemed as being out of control at the age of 14. I saw her once a week when she was in her thirties, married to an abusive man with a son who was beginning to identify with his father. At the time I did not have the experience, supervision or training to really help me make a difference. Cora would fill up her sessions with talk about foodstuffs that I could not help her think about in a meaningful way. I could not find a way of talking to her about what she was doing to her and me in the session by this non-stop attack on meaning. Nowadays, I would think of this as an enactment and might try to make a link with the father–daughter abuse that was not stopped by a mother who looked on.

## Self-help

As mentioned in the introductory chapter, the self-help movement has been at the heart of bringing to light some of the issues in eating disorders and has traditionally often been linked with the women's movement. Today, the self-help movement has expanded beyond this kind of base and there are self-help organisations related to all the different eating disorders and associated problems. The Eating Disorders Association hosts a self-help network which will put people in touch with facilitators who can help set up a group in a locality. There are also telephone contacts and postal contacts possible. EDA also helps organise for men to help each other. While self-help organisations may offer some support, they are no substitute for professional help. Furthermore, the more negative or competitive feelings aroused in talking about eating disorders can be difficult to manage. Nonetheless they may have a role to play for some people.

## Families and friends

The internet is an outstanding invention when it comes to accessing information about eating disorders. Friends and families may be very concerned about an individual who will not seek professional help. The Eating Disorders Association gives a good range of advice and information about eating disorders in a friendly and informal style. It may help if concerned parties are able to get some background information to alleviate their worse fears. When someone has an eating disorder and they do not want to recognise it or seek help, there is no way that another person can broach the matter without causing hurt and upset. The concerns of the third party need to be taken seriously but quite often any idea of 'help' which has not been self-selected seems like an interference to the person with the eating disorder. In student communities it is quite common for a group of students to become concerned about a particular colleague. This can be quite tricky for a single-handed student counsellor, for example, who may have to support an anxious group while 'leaving the door open' for a possible self-referral later. The psychoanalytic theories outlined here have stressed the range of underlying conflicts which may be expressed by an eating disorder. One feature which has been emphasised is the fear of intrusion and its counterpart, a sense of lonely isolation. It can be helpful in talking to associates of someone with an eating disorder to underline the need for them to be support-ive but to take a 'hands off' approach. However, it is much easier for a psychotherapist or counsellor to stand back than it is for someone who is personally involved and the stress created for families and friends is very serious, and needs careful handling.

## Life-style choice

On the other hand, there are movements which advocate particular ways of eating or shapes of body as a life-style choice. Some of these have been banned from posting their websites on the internet by com-panies like 'Yahoo', after public outcries. Such websites use politicised language and the rationale of freedom of speech to promote whatever is their preference. They often disappear from the web after a short while only to reappear in another spot (Shade, 2003). They have names like *'Ana by Choice'* (pro-anorexia) and *'Mia by Choice'* (pro-bulimia) and seem to take pride in what some people feel ashamed about or depressed about. These kind of sites might be distasteful to some of us and some are even straightforwardly pornographic and, I presume, designed and written by pornographers. They seem to have little to do with the organisations such as EDA that seek to support and encourage people with eating disorders. However, the way in which an eating disorder can become a kind of identity holding together a vulnerable personality is similar. In self-help groups run by organisations the identity is more linked to trying to find other, more accepted ways of resolving difficulties and feeling empowered.

## Research

Researching eating disorders is big business and the research litera-ture on bulimia and obesity is catching up with the huge research base on anorexia. The future of much research looks geared up to finding 'evidence-based treatments' for eating disorders. This sounds meritorious and as I write, there is a consultation document on the internet, produced by the National Institute for Clinical Excellence, which very thoroughly maps out the treatment guidelines for eating disorders in the National Health Service in the UK. However, closer scrutiny reveals the enormous bias towards cognitive-behavioural approaches. While these may be effective in the short-term, it remains to be seen what outcomes there will be over a much longer period of time. Zerba (1993) who is an American psychiatrist and psychoanalyst with enormous experience in eating disorders advocates an integrative approach to treating eating disorders. She supports combining medication with cognitive behavioural therapy, psychodynamic therapy, nutritional counselling and group therapy in in-patient treatment centres. Yet she believes that eating disorders will remain a clinical challenge since at least a third of eating disorder patients remain 'severely ill at follow-up' (1993: 369).

This was borne out by Halmi *et al.* (1991), who did a ten year follow up study of 76 anorexics some 56 per cent of whom had multiple relapses. Research will probably help us identify better the particular kind of patients who may benefit from different treatments. For longer-term psychoanalytically informed treatments it means that there is a necessity to take part in research projects which compare our ways of working with patients to other treatment modalities. This means not only participating in random control trials in order to establish an evidence base which is credible but finding other convincing ways of proving that a psychoanalytic approach has special merits for some, if not for all patients. These are difficult issues for psychoanalytic practitioners whose ethos is to explore complexity and specificity rather than find a standard 'one size fits all' manualised treatment. It may be that a psychoanalytic approach will prove to be the treatment of choice for the most disturbed individuals and this has certainly been suggested by Johnson (1991) in relation to eating-disordered patients with borderline personality disorder.

## Cultural contexts revisited

I hope the discussions in this book and the clinical illustrations have worked together to support the idea that, above all, a psychoanalytic or psychodynamic approach should be open to what specific meanings can be attached to eating disorders as discovered in a dialogue with the patient – furthermore, a conversation which will be subjected to the stirring up of unconscious processes in both parties. Yet there are some general issues which do invite more analysis about the relationship between eating disorders and culture. This is problematic for clinicians who have been accused of being glib and unsophisticated in understanding links with the non-clinical, yet vital if social theory is to be properly clinically informed (Swartz, 2001). Collaboration is of benefit to cultural and social analysts and clinicians, not to mention patients! The contradictory, but nonetheless, apparent increases in some parts of the world of eating disorders disprove the notion that once prevailed that anorexia, in particular, was a 'white' middle-class disorder of girls in the West. This 'perception' prevented anorexia being diagnosed in people who did not fit the description and really needed some help, as the quotation from the young man whose GP could not believe a man could be anorexic, showed.

Yet we also need to be cautious about medicalising or psychologising trends that may reflect the bias of researchers' interests or be inadequately understood. Readers may be aware of a push in the USA to market Viagra for women: a new category of female sexual dissatisfaction is being constructed in order to provide an outlet for the product according to some experts in the field (Tiefer, 2003). We should beware trying to create a similar 'eating disorder therapy consumer' where it is not appropriate. To fully understand the cultural dimensions of eating disorders we need to respect the subtlety and complexity of approaches that come from diverse disciplines. For example, there is a body of research about how media messages are 'read' which subverts the simplistic idea that we simply passively receive what the media tell us. For example, Varan (1998) suggests that the common belief that media systems act as vehicles for cultural imperialism needs to be balanced with research on how communities read and use what is broadcast in television. He used the metaphor of erosion of values in a study which showed that communities may actively use television in a host of ways, and that the consequences can be a strengthening of the local cultural values over time, not an erosion. When we look at cultural dimensions we need to beware the trap of turning active, passionate, albeit sometimes disturbed and disturbing, individuals into mere victims of society. Van Esterik proposed a different kind of research to the evidence-based one mentioned above, in relation to the cultural context of eating disorders:

> To tackle problems like eating disorders, interdisciplinary research between anthropologists and psychologists is now necessary. Take

us on board and we will help bridge the gap between macro level explanations for eating disorders such as globalisation, individualisation or gender oppression, and individual pathologies, and perhaps suggest some of the mechanisms linking the two. (2001: 22)

Falk's work may be of relevance here – we join in with a practice that benefits the consumer culture when we become dissatisfied with our bodies and work on them. We become affiliated. Talk to most women about dieting and we discover an emotional lingua franca. Obesity is of interest in this respect: it has gone from being a problem of the rich to a problem of the poor (though not of the very poor who still starve to death). Obesity is a class issue as well as a therapeutic and health issue. The Association for the Study of Obesity suggests:

Historically, obesity was associated with affluence and this is still the case across societies. Within developing countries such as India, Africa and South America obesity is a particular problem amongst the recently affluent classes, where being overweight is seen as a sign of prosperity. However, in developed countries there is an inverse relationship between obesity and social class, with a much greater proportion of obese people in the lower social classes than in professional groups. In the UK the prevalence of serious obesity in women increases from 15.1% in social class I to 31.4% in social class V. (June 2000: These figures are the latest on the prevalence of obesity from the 1998 Health Survey for England, published by the Department of Health.) (The Association for the Study of Obesity, 2003)

Globalisation has both negative and positive characteristics: if the dominant ideology is capitalist then to compete successfully and to bear the signs of a successful life will involve participating in consumerism, while displaying a self and body that has been worked on and shows no evidence of 'laissez-faire'. Or we can take a more measured approach and help our patients resist such oversimplifications – not by promoting any particular body shape or practice, but by helping them establish real relationships with themselves and real other people who are not commodified. This is, of course, a paradox for the psychotherapies, which may have become seen as part of the individualised, consumerist approach to well-being. Nevertheless, psychoanalytically orientated help is essential for some, as I hope this book has shown.

Some key points

- Psychic retreats may hide the deeper pathology of a patient in treatment.
- Psychotic functioning may be involved in the more severe cases of eating disorders.
- The capacity to symbolise may be impaired.
- A common defence mechanism may be negation.
- Mental space may be restricted in the patient and the therapy.
- Psychosomatic disorders are often found in people with eating disorders, especially Irritable Bowel Syndrome.
- Self-harm may be present in a non-eating related form.
- Vulnerability to sexual abuse may be a factor whether it has actually taken place or is a fear about intimacy linked to the phantasy of intrusion.
- Self-help, although of limited usefulness, is nonetheless important.
- Families and friends may need support.
- Research may identify which patients do best with a psychoanalytic approach.
- The complexity of the cultural context should not obscure the importance of individual pathology and the need for a psychoanalytic approach.

# Additional Information

## Useful addresses, telephone numbers and websites

www.adiosbarbie.com
(An antidote to the cult of thinness)

www.aso.org.uk
(Association for the Study of Obesity)

Eating Disorders Association
103 Prince of Wales Road
Norwich
NR1 1DW
United Kingdom
Adult Helpline: 0845 634 1414 (open 8:30 to 20:30 weekdays)
Youthline: 0845 6347650 (open 16:00 to 18:30 weekdays)
Text-phone Service: 01603 753322 (open 8:30 to 20:30 weekdays)
Helpline email service helpmail @edauk.com
Administrative email: info@edauk.com

www.nice.org.uk
(National Institute for Clinical Excellence)

www.repsych.ac.uk
(Royal College of Psychiatrists)

# REFERENCES

Alexander, F. (1934) 'The influence of psychological factors upon gastrointestinal disturbances', *Psychoanalytic Quarterly*. 3: 501–39.

Allebeck, P., D. Hallberg *et al.* (1976) 'Body-image – An apparatus for measuring disturbances in estimation of size and shape', *Journal of Psychosomatic Research*. 26: 583–9.

American Psychiatric Association (1994) *Diagnostic and Statistical Manual of Mental Disorders*. Washington, USA: American Psychiatric Association.

Andersen, E. A. and Bowers, W. A. (1999) 'Males, gender and eating disorders – risk bias and treatment outcome', *Fourth International Eating Disorders Conference*. London, April.

Anderson, R. (2001) 'The language of the body in adolescence', *Eating Disorders Conference*. London: Institute of Psychoanalysis, October.

Anderson, R. and A. Dartington (eds) [1998] *Facing it out: clinical perspectives on adolescent disturbance*. London: Duckworth. Reprinted, London: Karnac, 2002.

Askevold, E. (1975) 'Measuring body image: preliminary report of a new method', *Psychother Psychosom*. 26: 71–7.

Baker, R. (1993) 'The patient's discovery of the psychoanalyst as a new object', *International Journal of Psycho-Analysis*. 74: 1223–33.

Barret, D. and Fine, H. J. (1990) 'The gnostic syndrome: Anorexia nervosa', *Psychoanalytic Psychotherapy*. 4: 263–70.

Becker, A. E., Burwell, R. A., Gilman, S. E., Herzog, D. B. and Hamburg, P. (2002) 'Eating behaviours and attitudes following prolonged exposure to television among fijian adolescent girls', *British Journal of Psychiatry*. 180: 509–14.

Bell, R. (1985) *Holy Anorexia*. Chicago: University of Chicago Press.

Bemporad, J. R. and Herzog, D. B. (1989) *Psychoanalysis and Eating Disorders*. New York: Guilford Press.

Berlin, I. N., Boatman, M. J., Sheimo, S. L. and Szurek, S. A. (1951) 'Adolescent alternation of anorexia and obesity', *American Journal of Orthopsychiatry*. 21: 387–419.

Bick, E. (1968) 'The experience of the skin in early object relations', *International Journal of Psycho-Analysis*. 49: 484–6.

Bion, W. R. (1962) *Learning from Experience*. London: Heinemann.

Bion, W. R. (1957) 'Differentiation of the psychotic from the non-psychotic personalities', *International Journal of Psycho-Analysis*. 38: 266–75.

Bion, W. R. (1967) 'Differentiation of the psychotic from non-psychotic personalities', in *Second Thoughts*. London: Karnac. 43–63.

Birksted-Breen, D. (1989) 'Working with an anorexic patient', *International Journal of Psycho-Analysis*. 70: 29–40.

Birksted-Breen, D. (1996) 'Phallus, penis and mental space', *International Journal of Psycho-Analysis*. 77: 649–57.

Bordo, S. (1993b) *Unbearable Weight: Feminism, Western Culture and the Body*. Berkely: University of California.

Boris, H. (1984) 'The problem of anorexia nervosa', *International Journal of Psycho-Analysis*. 65: 315–22.

Boskind-White, M. and White, W. C. [1987] *Bulimarexia: The Binge/Purge Cycle*. New York: Norton. Reprinted, 1991.

Brennan, T. (1993) *History After Lacan*. London: Routledge.

Breuer, J. and Freud, S. (1893–95) 'Studies on hysteria', *Standard Edition*. 2: 1–305.

Britton, R. S. (1989) 'The missing link: Parental sexuality in the Oedipus complex', in Britton, R. S., Feldman, M. and E. O. O' Shaughnessy, *The Oedipus Complex Today*. London: Karnac.

Brodie, D. A., K. Bagley *et al.* (1994) 'Body-image perception in pre- and postadolescent females', *Perceptual and Motor Skills*. 78:147–54.

Bruch, H. (1957) *The Importance of Overweight*. New York: Norton.

Bruch, H. (1962) 'Perceptual and conceptual disturbances in anorexia nervosa', *Psychosomatic Medicine*. 24: 187–94.

Bruch, H. (1966) 'Anorexia nervosa, and its differential diagnosis', *Journal of Nervous Mental Disorders*. 141: 555–64.

Bruch, H. (1969) 'Obesity and orality', *Contemporary Psychoanalysis*. 5: 129–43.

Bruch, H. (1970) 'Psychotherapy in primary anorexia nervosa', *Journal of Nervous Mental Disorders*. 150: 51–67.

Bruch, H. (1973) *Eating Disorders: Obesity, Anorexia Nervosa, and the Person Within*. New York: Basic Books.

Buree, B., D. Papageorgis *et al.* (1984) 'Body image perception and preference in anorexia nervosa', *Canadian Journal of Psychiatry*. 29 (7): 557–63.

Button, E. J., F. Fransella *et al.* (1977). 'A reappraisal of body perception disturbance in anorexia nervosa', *Psychological Medicine*. 51: 235–43.

Castelnuovo-Tedesco, P. and Risen, S. E. (1988) 'Anorexia nervosa: Theory and therapy – a new look at an old problem', *Journal of American Analytic Association*. 36: 153–61.

Castelnuovo-Tedesco, P. and Whisnant Reiser, L. (1988) 'Compulsive eating: Obesity and related phenomena', *Journal of American Analytic Association*. 36: 163–71.

Chatoor, I. (1991) 'Infantile anorexia nervosa: a developmental disorder of separation and individuation', in Bemporad, J. R. and D. B. Herzog, *Psychoanalysis and Eating Disorders*. New York: Guilford Press.

Chatoor, I. and Egon, J. (1983) 'Nonorganic failure to thrive and dwarfism due to food refusal: a separation disorder'. *Journal of Academic Child Psychiatry*. 22: 294–301.

Chernin, K. (1983) *Womansize: Reflections on the Tyranny of Slenderness*. London: The Women's Press.

Chernin, K. (1985) *The Hungry Self. Women, Eating and Identity*. London: Virago Press.

Connors, M. E. and Morse, W. (1993) 'Sexual abuse and eating disorders: A review', *International Journal of Eating Disorders*. 13: 1–11.

Copperman, J. (2000) 'Eating disorders in the United Kingdom: Review of the provision of health care services for men with eating disorders'. London: Eating Disorders Association.

Crisp, A. H. (1980) *Anorexia Nervosa: Let Me Be*. New York: Academic Press.

Crisp, A. H. (2002) 'Editorial: A tale of corruption', *British Journal of Psychiatry*. 180: 480–2.

Crisp, A. H. and Kalucy, R. S. (1974) 'Aspects of the perceptual disorder in anorexia nervosa', *British Journal of Medical Psychology*. 47: 349–61.

Dally, P. and Gomez, J. (1980) *Obesity and Anorexia Nervosa: A Question of Shape*. London: Faber & Faber Ltd.

Dennis, A. B. and Sansone, R. A. (1991) 'The clinical stages of treatment for the eating disorder patient with borderline personality disorder', in C. Johnson (ed.), *Psychodynamic Treatment of Anorexia Nervosa and Bulimia*. New York: Guilford Press. 128–64.

DOH (1999) *A National Service Framework for Mental Health*. London: Stationery Office.

Durkheim, E. [1897] *Suicide: a Study in Sociology*. London: Routledge and Kegan Paul. Reprinted, 1970.

Ernst, S. and Goodison, L. (eds) (1981) *In Our Own Hands. A Book of Self-Help Therapy*. London: The Women's Press.

Falk, P. (1994) *The Consuming Body*. London: Sage.

Fairbairn, W. R. D. (1952) *Psychoanalytic Studies of the Personality*. London: Tavistock.

Falstein, E. I., Feinstein, S. C. and Judas, I. (1956) 'Anorexia in the male child', *American Journal of Orthopsychiatry*. 26: 751–72.

Farrell, E. (1995) *Lost for Words*. London: Process Press.

Farrell, E. (2003) Personal communication.

Fenichel, O. (1945) *Psychoanalytic Theory of Neurosis*. New York: Norton.

Fisher, G. H. (1973) 'But if they either are not what they seem, or seem what they are not, then how can perceptual distortions be measured?', *Perception*. 2: 165–6.

*Flanders, S. (2001)* 'Adolescent conflict and eating disorders', *Eating Disorders Conference*. London: Institute of Psychoanalysis, October.

Fombonne, E. (1995) 'Anorexia nervosa: No evidence of an increase', *British Journal of Psychiatry*. 166: 462–71.

Fonagy, P. (ed.) (1999) 'Reflections on psychoanalytic research problems – An anglo-saxon view', in *An Open Door Review of Outcome Studies in Psychoanalysis*. London: Research Committee of the International Psychoanalytic Association.

Foucault, M. (1979) *Discipline and Punish. The Birth of the Prison*. Harmondsworth: Penguin Books.

Freeman, R. J., C. D. Thomas *et al.* (1984) 'A modified video camera for measuring body image distortion: Technical description and reliability', *Psychological Medicine*. 2: 411–16.

Freud, A. (1972) 'The psychoanalytic study of infantile eating disorders', in Harrison, S. and J. McDermitt (eds), *Childhood Psychopathology*. New York: International Universities Press.

Freud, S. (1899) 'Extracts from the Fliess papers', in J. Strachey (ed.), *The Standard Edition of the Complete Psychological Works of Sigmund Freud*. 1: 175–280. London: Hogarth Press.

Freud, S. (1905) 'Three essays on the theory of sexuality', in *Standard Edition*. 7: 125–249. London: Hogarth Press.

Freud, S. [1911] 'Psychoanalyical notes on an account of a case of paranoia (Dementia Paranoides)', in *Standard Edition*. 12: 1–82. London: Hogarth Press. Reprinted, 1958.

Freud, S. (1920) 'Beyond the pleasure principle', in *Standard Edition*. 18: 1–64. London: Hogarth Press.

Freud, S. (1924) 'Neurosis and psychosis', in *Standard Edition*. 19: 147–53. London: Hogarth Press.

Freud, S. (1925) 'Negation', in *Standard Edition*. 19: 233–9. London: Hogarth Press.

Gardner, F. (2001) *Self-Harm: A Psychotherapeutic Approach*. Hove: Brunner-Routledge.

Garner, D. M., P. E. Garfinkel *et al.* (1976) 'Body image disturbance in anorexia nervosa and obesity', *Psychosomatic Medicine*. 38: 3327–36.

Garner, D. M. and Garfinkel, P. E. (1981–82) 'Body image in anorexia nervosa: measurement, theory and clinical implications', *Psychiatry Medicine*. 11: 263–84.

Garner, D., Garfinkel, P., Schwartz, D. and Thompson, M. (1980) 'Cultural expectation of thinness in women', *Psychological Reports*. 47: 483–91.

Gehrie, M. (1985) 'Comment on eating disorders: Dynamics and treatment', Annual Meeting of American Psychoanalytic Association, Denver, 1985. Reported in Castelnuovo-Tedesco, P. and S. E. Risen (1988) 'Anorexia nervosa: Theory and therapy – a new look at an old problem', *Journal of American Analytic Association*. 36: 153–61.

Geist, R. A. (1989) 'Self psychological reflections on the origins of eating disorders' in Bemporad, J. R. and D. B. Herzog (eds) (1989) *Psychoanalysis and Eating Disorders*. (1989) New York: Guilford Press. 5–27.

Glucksman, M. L. (1989) 'Obesity: A psychoanalytic challenge', in Bemporad, J. R. and D. B. Herzog (eds) (1989) *Psychoanalysis and Eating Disorders*. (1989) New York: Guilford Press. 151–71.

Glucksman, M. L. and Hirsch, J. (1969) 'The response of obese patients to weight reduction: III. The perception of body size', *Psychosomatic Medicine*. 31: 1–7.

Goodsitt, A. (1983) 'Self-regulatory disturbances in eating disorders', *International Journal of Eating Disorders*. 2: 51–6.

Gordon, R. A. (1990) *Eating Disorders: Anatomy of a Social Epidemic*. Oxford: Blackwell. Reprinted, 2000.

Gordon, R. A. (2001) 'Eating disorders east and west: A culture-bound syndrome unbound', in Nasser, M., Katzman, M. A. and R. A. Gordon (eds), *Eating Disorders and Cultures in Transition*. Hove and New York: Brunner-Routledge. 1–16.

Gordon, R. and Neal, N. (1998) 'Is the prevalence of eating disorders declining among college students? A partial replication', *Eighth New York International Conference on Eating Disorders*. New York.

Grinberg, L. (1956) 'La negación en el comer compulsivo y en la obesidad', *Revista de Psicoanálisis*. 13 (2): 160–9.

Grinberg, L. (1992) *Guilt and Depression*. London and New York: Karnac.

Gull, W. W. (1873) 'Apepsia hysterica: Anorexia hysterica', *Transcripts of the Clinical Society of London*. 7: 22–8.

Gunew, S. (2001) 'Commentary 2' in Nasser, M., Katzman, M. A. and R. A. Gordon (eds), *Eating Disorders and Cultures in Transition*. Hove and New York: Brunner-Routledge: 168–70.

Habermas, T. (1990) *Heisshunger. Historische Bedingungen Der Bulimia Nervosa*. Frankfurt: Fischer.

Halmi, K. A. and Cunningham, S. (1977) 'Perceptual distortion of body image in adolescent girls; distortion of body image in adolescence', *Psychological Medicine*. 7: 253–57.

Hamburg, P. (1989) 'Bulimia: Construction of a symptom', in Bemporad, R. J. and D. B. Herzog (eds), *Psychoanalysis and Eating Disorders*. New York: Guilford Press. 131–40.

Harris, E. C. and Barraclough, B. (1998) 'Excess mortality of mental disorder', *British Journal of Psychiatry*. 173: 11–53.

Heatherton, T. F., Nichols, P., Mahamedi, F. and Keel, P. (1995) 'Body weight, dieting and eating disorders symptoms among college strudents, 1982–1992', *American Journal of Psychiatry*. 152: 1623–9.

Horne, R. L., J. C. Van Vactor *et al*. (1991). 'Disturbed body image in patients with eating disorders', *American Journal of Psychiatry*. 148 (2): 211–15.

Hsu, G. L. K. (1990) *Eating Disorders*. New York: Guilford Press.

Hsu, L. K. G. (1997) 'Can dieting cause an eating disorder?', *Psychological Medicine*. 27: 509–13.

Hughes, A., Furgiuele, P. and Bianco, M. (1985) 'Aspects of anorexia nervosa in the therapy of two adolescents', *Journal of Child Psychotherapy*. 11 (1): 17–32.

Jessner, J. and Abse, D. W. (1960) 'Regressive forces in anorexia nervosa', *British Journal of Medical Psychology*. 33: 301–12.

Johnson, C. (ed.) (1991) *Psychodynamic Treatment of Anorexia Nervosa and Bulimia*. New York: Guilford Press. 128–64.

Kalliopuska, M. (1982) 'Body image disturbance in patients with anorexia nervosa', *Psychological Reports*. 51: 715–22.

Kaufman, R. M. and M. Heiman (eds) (1964) *Evolution of Psychosomatic Concepts. Anorexia nervosa: A Paradigm*. New York: International Universities Press.

Kearney-Cooke, A. (1991) 'The role of the therapist in the treatment of eating disorders: A feminist psychodynamic approach', in Johnson, C. (1991) *Psychodynamic Treatment of Anorexia Nervosa and Bulimia*. New York: Guilford Press. 295–318.

Kestenberg, J. (1968) 'Outside and inside, male and female', *Journal of American Psychoanalytic Association*. 16: 457–520.

Klein, M. [1952] 'Some theoretical conclusions regarding the emotional life of the infant', in *Envy and Gratitude*. New York: Dell Publishing (1975) 61–93.

Kohon, G. (ed.) (1999) *The Dead Mother: The Work of André Green*. London and New York: Routledge.

Krueger, D. W. (1988) 'Body self, psychological self and bulimia: Developmental and clinical considerations', in Schwartz, H. J. (ed.) (1988) *Bulimia: Psychoanalytic Treatment and Theory*. Connecticut: International Universities Press. 55–73.

Lasegue, C. (1873) 'On hysterical anorexia', in Kaufman, R. M. and M. Heiman (eds) (1964) *Evolution of Psychosomatic Concepts. Anorexia Nervosa: A Paradigm*. New York: International Universities Press. 141–55.

Lask, B. and Bryant-Waugh, R. (eds) (2000) *Anorexia Nervosa and Related Eating Disorders in Childhood and Adolescence*. London: Psychology Press.

Laufer, M. and Laufer, M. E. (1984) *Adolescence and Adolescent Breakdown: A Psychoanalytic View*. New Haven, CT: Yale University Press. Reprinted, London: Karnac, 1995.

Lawrence, M. (1984) *The Anorexic Experience*. London: The Women's Press.

Lawrence, M. (ed.) (1987) *Fed Up and Hungry. Women, Oppression and Food*. London: The Women's Press.

Lawrence, M. (2002) 'Body, mind, mother. Anorexia, femininity and the intrusive object', *International Journal of Psycho-Analysis*. 83: 837–50.

Lee, S. (2001) 'Fat phobia in anorexia nervosa: Whose obsession is it?', in Nasser, M., Katzman, M. A. and R. A. Gordon (eds), *Eating Disorders and Cultures in Transition*. Hove and New York: Brunner-Routledge. 40–54.

Lefebvre, H. (1974) *The Production of Space*. Trans. Nicholson-Smith, Oxford: Blackwell, 1991, reprinted 1994.

Lefebvre, P. (1991) 'Review of H. J. Schwartz (ed.) (1988) "Bulimia: Psychoanalytic treatment and theory" ', *Psychoanalytic Quarterly*. 60: 474–9.

Levy, I. and Adams, B. D. (1998) 'Early unwanted sexual experiences, obsessionality and eating disorders', *Counselling Psychology Review*. 13 (2): 4–12.

Littlewood, R. (2001) 'Commentary 1', in Nasser, M., Katzman, M. A. and R. A. Gordon (eds), *Eating Disorders and Cultures in Transition*. Hove and New York: Brunner-Routledge: 55–60.

Lloyd, T. (1997) *Men's Health Review*. Men's Health Forum/Royal College of Nursing, London.

MacSween, M. (1993) *Anorexic Bodies: A Feminist and Sociological Perspective on Anorexia Nervosa*. London: Routledge.

Main, T. (1957) 'The ailment', *British Journal of Medical Psychology*. 30: 129–45.

Main, M. and Solomon, J. (1986) 'Discovery of a new, insecure – disorganised/disoriented attachment pattern', in Yogman, M. and T. B. Brazelton (eds), *Affective Development in Infancy*. Norwood, NJ: Ablex Press. 95–124.

Malson, H. (1998) *The Thin Woman: Feminism, Post-Structuralism and the Social Psychology of Anorexia Nervosa*. London: Routledge.

McDougall, J. (1989) *Theatres of the Body: a Psychoanalytical Approach to Psychosomatic Illness*. London: Free Association Books.

Meerman, R. (1983) 'Experimental investigation of disturbances in body image estimation in anorexia nervosa patients and ballet and gymnastic pupils', *International Journal of Eating Disorders*. 2 (4): 91–100.

Meltzer, D. (1975) 'Dimensionality as a parameter of mental functioning: its relation to narcissistic organisation', in Meltzer, D., Bremner, J., Hoxter, S., Wedell, D. and I. Wittenberg, *Explorations in Autism*. Strathtay: Cluny Press. 223–38.

Menzies, I. E. P. (1970) 'Psychosocial aspects of eating', *Journal of Psychosomatic Research*. 14: 223–7.

Mennell, S. (1985) *All Manners of Food*. Oxford: Blackwell.

Meyer, D. C. and Weinroth, L. A. (1957) 'Observations on psychological aspects of anorexia nervosa', *Psychosomatic Medicine*. 19: 389–93.

Milton, J. (1997) 'Why assess? Psychoanalytic assessment in the NHS', *Psychoanalytic Psychotherapy*. 11 (1): 47–58.

Minuchin, S., Rosman, B. L. and Baker, L. (1978) *Psychosomatic Families: Anorexia Nervosa in Context*. Cambridge, Mass: Harvard University Press.

Modell, A. (1980) 'Affects and their non-communication', *International Journal of Psycho-Analysis*. 61: 259–67.

Nasser, M. (1997) *Culture and Weight Consciousness*. London: Routledge.

Nasser, M., Katzman, M. A. and R. A. Gordon (eds) (2001) *Eating Disorders and Cultures in Transition*. Hove and New York: Brunner-Routledge.

Norris, D. L. (1984) 'The effects of mirror confrontation on self-estimation of body dimensions in anorexia nervosa, bulimia and two control groups', *Psychological Medicine*. 14 (4): 835–42.

Oliner, M. (1982) 'The anal phase', in Mendell, D. (ed.) *Early Female Development*. New York: SP Medical and Scientific Press. 25–60.

Orbach, S. (1978) *Fat is a Feminist Issue*. New York and London: Paddington Press.

Orbach, S. (1986) *Hunger Strike: The Anorectic's Struggle as a Metaphor for Our Age*. London: Faber and Faber.

Palmer, R. (2001) 'Commentary 1', in Nasser, M., Katzman, M. A. and R. A. Gordon (eds), *Eating Disorders and Cultures in Transition*. Hove and New York: Brunner-Routledge: 17–19.

Penner, L. A., J. K. Thompson *et al.* (1991) 'Size overestimation among anorexics: Much ado about very little?', *Journal of Abnormal Psychology*. 100 (1): 90–3.

Perelberg, R. J. and Levinson, N. A. (2003) Panel on 'Acting out and/or enactment', *International Journal of Psychoanalysis*. 84, Part I: 151–5.

Pierloot, R. A. and Houben, M. E. (1978) 'Estimation of body dimensions in anorexia nervosa', *Psychological Medicine*. 8: 317–24.

Polivy, J. and Herman, C. P. (1985) 'Dieting and bingeing: A causal analysis', *American Psychologist*. 40: 193–201.

Pope, H. G., Katz, D. L. and Hudson, J. I. (1993) 'Anorexia nervosa and "Reverse Anorexia" among 108 male bodybuilders', *Comprehensive Psychiatry*. 34 (6): 406–9.

Probst, M., H. Van Coppenolle *et al.* (1992) 'Body image asessment in anorexia nervosa patients and university students by means of video distortion: A reliability study', *Journal of Psychosomatic Research*. 36 (1): 89–97.

Rathner, G. (2001) 'Post communism and the marketing of the thin ideal' in Nasser, M., Katzman, M. A. and R. A. Gordon (eds), *Eating Disorders and Cultures in Transition*. Hove and New York: Brunner-Routledge: 93–104.

Rathner, G., Tury, F., Szabo, P., Geyer, H., Runpold, G., Forgaces, A., Sollner, W. and Plotnner, G. (1995) 'Prevalence of eating disorders and minor psychiatric morbidity in Central Europe before the political changes in 1989: A cross-cultural study', *Psychological Medicine*. 5: 1027–35.

Ravussin, E., Lillioja, S., Knowler, W. C., Christin, L., Freymond, D., Abbott, W. G. H., Boyce, V. and Bogardus, C. (1988) 'Reduced rate of energy expenditure as a risk factor for body weight gain', *New England Journal of Medicine*. 318: 467–72.

Read, N. (2000) 'Why does the gut express the grievance?', *Conference on Linking Mind–Body–Culture Psychoanalytically*. University of Sheffield, June.

Reich, G. (1997) 'Psychodynamische aspekte der bulimie und anorexie' in Reich, G. and M. Cierpka (eds), *Die Psychotherapie der Esstörungen*. Stuttgart: Thieme.

Reich, G. and Cierpka, M. (1998) 'Identity conflicts in bulimia nervosa: Psychodynamic patterns and psychoanalytic treatment', *Psychoanalytic Inquiry*. 18: 382–402.

Rey, H. (1994) *Universals of Psychoanalysis in the Treatment of Psychotic and Borderline States: Factors of Space-Time and Language*. London: Free Association Books.

Rizzuto, A-M. (1988) 'Transference, language, and affect in the treatment of bulimarexia', *International Journal of Psycho-Analysis*. 69: 369–87.

Rouah, A. (1980) 'Anorexia nervosa', *Psychotherapia*. 6: 17–25.

Roberts, S. B., Savage, J., Coward, W., Chew, B. and Lucas, A. (1988) 'Energy expenditure and intake in infants born to lean and overweight mothers', *New England Journal of Medicine*. 318: 461–6.

Rosenfeld, H. (1972) 'A critical appreciation of James Strachey's paper "On the nature of the therapeutic action of psychoanalysis"' (postscript). *International Journal of Psychoanalysis*. 53: 455–61.

Royal College of Psychiatrists (2000) 'Eating disorders in the UK: Policies for service development and training'. Report from the Eating Disorders Special Interest Group of the Royal College of Psychiatrists, London.

Russell, G. (1979) 'Bulimia nervosa: An ominous variant of anorexia nervosa', *Psychological Medicine*. 9: 429–48.

Sachs, H. (1929) 'One of the motive factors in the formation of the superego in women', *International Journal of Psycho-Analysis*. 110: 39–50.

Schmidt, U., Humfress, H. and Treasure, J. (1997) 'The role of general family environment and sexual and physical abuse in the origins of eating disorders', *Eating Disorders Review*. 5 (3): 184–207.

Schneider, J. A. (1991) 'Gender identity issues in male bulimia nervosa', in C. Johnson (ed.) (1991) *Psychodynamic Treatment of Anorexia Nervosa and Bulimia*. New York: Guilford Press. 194–222.

Schwartz, H. J. (1986) 'Bulimia: Psychoanalytic perspectives', *Journal of American Psychoanalytic Association*. 34: 439–62.

Schwartz, H. J. (ed.) (1988) *Bulimia: Psychoanalytic Treatment and Theory*. Connecticut: International Universities Press.

Segal, H. (1978) 'On symbolism', *International Journal of Psycho-Analysis*. 59: 315–19.

Segal, H. (1957) 'Notes on symbol formation', *International Journal of Psycho-Analysis*. 38: 391–7.

Selvini-Palazzoli, M. (1974) *Self-Starvation: from the Individual to Family Therapy in the Treatment of Anorexia Nervosa*. Reprinted, New York: Jason Aronson, 1978.

Shade, L. R. (2003) 'Weborexics: The ethical issues surrounding pro-ana websites', *Computer Ethics Philosophical Enquiry Conference*. Boston, USA.

Shipton, G. (1999) 'Anorexic space', *Journal of Community and Applied Social Psychology*. 9: 435–48.

Shipton, G. and Smith, E. (1998) *Long-term Counselling*. London: Sage.

Slade, P. D. and Russell, G. F. M. (1973) 'Awareness of body dimension in anorexia nervosa: Cross-sectional and longitudinal studies', *Psychological Medicine*. 3: 188–99.

Sohn, L. (1985) 'Anorexic and bulimic states of mind in the psycho-analytic treatment of anorexic/bulimic patients and psychotic patients', *Psychoanalytic Psychotherapy*. 1 (2): 49–56.

Sours, J. A. (1969) 'Anorexia nervosa: Nosology, diagnosis, developmental patterns, and power-control dynamics', in Caplan, G. and S. Lebovici (eds), *Adolescence: Psychosocial Perspectives*. New York: Basic Books.

Sours, J. A. (1974) 'The anorexia nervosa syndrome', *International Journal of Psycho-Analysis*. 55: 567–76.

Sours, J. A. (1980) *Starving to death in a Sea of Objects. The Anorexia Nervosa Syndrome*. New York and London: Jason Aronson.

Sperling, M. (1983) 'A re-evaluation of classification, concepts, and treatment', in Wilson, C. (ed.), *Fear of Being Fat*. New York and London: Jason Aronson.

Spillius, E. B. (2002) 'Understanding oneself and being understood: Experiences of supervising psychoanalysts and psychotherapists', *Psychoanalysis in Europe Bulletin*. 56: 5–16.

Sprince, M. (1984) 'Early psychic disturbance in anorexic and bulimic patients as reflected in the psychoanalytic process', *Journal of Child Psychotherapy*. 10: 199–215.

Sprince, M. (1988) 'Experiencing and recovering transitional space in the analytic treatment of anorexia nervosa and bulimia', in Schwartz, H. J. (ed.) (1988) *Bulimia: Psychoanalytic Treatment and Theory*. Connecticut: International Universities Press. 73–89.

Steiner, J. (1993) *Psychic Retreats. Pathological Organizations in Psychotic, Neurotic and Borderline Patients*. London and New York: Routledge.

Stiglitz, J. (2002) *Globalization and its Discontents*. London and New York: Penguin Books.

Stolorow, R. D., Brandchaft, B. and Atwood, G. E. (1987) *Psychoanalytic Treatment: An Intersubjective Approach*. Hillsdale, N.J.: Analytic Press.

Strachey, J. (1969) 'The nature of the therapeutic action of psychoanalysis', *International Journal of Psychoanalysis*. 50: 275–92. Reprinted from *International Journal of Psychoanalysis*. 1934, 15: 127–59.

Strober, M. (1991) 'Disorders of the self in anorexia nervosa: An organismic – developmental paradigm', in Johnson, C. (ed.) (1991) *Psychodynamic Treatment of Anorexia Nervosa and Bulimia*. New York: Guilford Press. 354–73.

Sugarman, A. and Kurash, C. (1981) 'The body as a transitional object in bulimia', *International Journal of Eating Disorders*. 14: 57–66.

Swartz, L. (2001) Commentary 1, in Nasser, M., Katzman, M. A. and R. A. Gordon (eds), *Eating Disorders and Cultures in Transition*. Hove and New York: Brunner-Routledge. 34–6.

Swift, W. J. (1991) 'Bruch revisited: The role of interpretation of transference and resistance in the psychotherapy of eating disorders', in Johnson, C. (ed.) (1991) *Psychodynamic Treatment of Anorexia Nervosa and Bulimia*. New York: Guilford Press. 51–67.

Temple, N. (2003) Psychosomatic medicine and psychoanalysis, Seminar, Institute of Psychoanalysis, London.

Thomä, H. (1967) *Anorexia Nervosa*. New York: International Universities Press.

Thorner, H. A. (1970) 'On compulsive eating', *Journal of Psychosomatic Research*. 14: 321–5.

Tiefer, L. (2003) 'The pink viagra story: We have the drug, but what's the disease?', *Radical Philosophy*. 121: 2–5.

Tobin, D. L. and Johnson, C. (1991) 'The integration of psychodynamic and behaviour therapy in the treatment of eating disorders: clinical issues versus theoretical mystique', in Johnson, C. (1991) Psychodynamic Treatment of Anorexia Nervosa and Bulimia. New York: Guilford Press. 374–97.

Truby, H. and Paxton, S. J. (2002) 'Development of the children's body image scale', British Journal of Clinical Psychology. 41: 185–203.

Turner, B. S. (1984) The Body and Society. Oxford: Blackwell, Second edition, London: Sage, 1996.

Van Esterik, P. (2001) 'Commentary 2', in Nasser, M., Katzman, M. A. and R. A. Gordon (eds), Eating Disorders and Cultures in Transition. Hove and New York: Brunner-Routledge. 20–3.

Varan, D. (1998) 'The cultural erosion metaphor and the transcultural impact of media systems', Journal of Communication. 48: 58–85.

Waller, J. V., Kaufman, M. R. and Deutsch, F. (1940) 'Anorexia nervosa: A psychosomatic entity', in Kaufman, R. M. and M. Heiman (eds) (1964) Evolution of Psychosomatic Concepts. Anorexia Nervosa: A Paradigm. New York: International Universities Press. 145–276.

Wallop, H. (2003) 'Fat is a shareholder issue', Investors Chronicle. 145/1841: 18–21.

Warah, A. (1989) 'Body image disturbance in anorexia nervosa: Beyond body image', Canadian Journal of Psychiatry. 34: 898–905.

Whitehouse, A. M., C. P. L. Freeman et al. (1988) 'Body size estimation in anorexia nervosa', British Journal of Psychiatry. 153 (Suppl 2): 23–6.

Williams, G. (1997) Internal Landscapes and Foreign Bodies. Eating Disorders and Other Pathologies. London: Duckworth.

Williams, G. (1998) 'Reflections on some particular dynamics of eating disorders', in Anderson, R. and A. Dartington (eds) (1998) Facing it Out: Clinical Perspectives on Adolescent Disturbance. London: Duckworth. Reprinted, London: Karnac. 79–97.

Wilson, P. (1992) Psychodynamic Technique in the Treatment of Eating Disorders. New York: Jason Aronson.

Wingate, B. A. and Christie, M. J. (1978) 'Ego strength and body image in anorexia nervosa', Journal of Psychosomatic Research. 22: 201–4.

Winnicott, D. W. (1947) 'Hate in the countertransference', in Through Paediatrics to Psychoanalysis. London: Karnac. 194–303.

Winnicott, D. W. (1960) 'Countertransference', British Journal of Medical Psychology. 33: 17–21.

Woodmansey, A. C. (1966) 'The internalization of external conflict', International Journal of Psycho-Anaysis. 47: 349–55.

Wooley, S. C. (1991) 'Uses of countertransference in the treatment of eating disorders: a gender perspective', in Johnson, C. (1991) Psychodynamic Treatment of Anorexia Nervosa and Bulimia. New York: Guilford Press. 245–94.

World Health Organisation (1992) The ICD-10 Classification of Mental and Behavioural Disorders. Geneva: WHO.

Wouters, C. (1977) 'Informalisierung und der Prozess der Zivilizasion' in P. Gleichmann et al. (eds), Materialien zu Norbert Elias' Zivilisationtheorie. Frankfurt am Main: Suhrkamp: 279–98.

Young, R. (1994) Mental Space. London: Free Association Books.

Zerbe, K. J. (1993) The Body Betrayed: Women, Eating Disorders and Treatment. Washington, DC and London: American Psychiatric Press.

# INDEX